JAGUARS IN COMPETITION

JAGUARS IN COMPETITION

Chris Harvey

Foreword by Stirling Moss

OSPREY

Published in 1979 by Osprey Publishing Limited,
12–14 Long Acre, London WC2E 9LP
Member company of the George Philip Group

United States distribution by

Motorbooks International
Publishers & Wholesalers Inc

Osceola, Wisconsin 54020, USA

British Library Cataloguing in Publication Data

Harvey, Chris
Jaguars in competition.
1. Automobile racing
2. Automobile rallies
3. Jaguar automobile
I. Title
796.7′2 GV1029.15

ISBN 0 85045 323 2

Editor Tim Parker

Design Peter Wrigley

Filmset and printed in Great Britain by
BAS Printers Limited, Over Wallop, Hampshire

Contents

JAGUARS IN COMPETITION

Chris Harvey

Foreword

When I was asked to write this foreword, I began to consider just what Jaguar cars had meant to me. The answer is just about everything that was good about the glorious post-war years of sports car racing; sensational vehicles, incredible braking and last, but by no means least, my good friend Tommy Wisdom, who had given me my first chance in big-time sports car racing. Sometime during 1950, Tommy had telephoned me and asked if I would like to drive his brand new, factory-prepared, privately entered, XK 120 in the classic Tourist Trophy. I was absolutely thrilled and jumped at the chance. Actually, it was even more exciting than it sounds, because all the manufacturers that I had approached for a drive had turned me down because they felt that I was driving a bit too quickly and would have an accident. And they did not want it happening in their car.

It was one of the worst days I can remember, with weather as vile as anybody could imagine. Torrential rain and a howling gale drove all but the toughest spectators to seek shelter, either in bogged-down cars, back at home or in the local bars. Tents and marquees were blown down and the paddock was a quagmire. Rivers of water and mud flowed down the roads but the police and marshals stuck to their posts; there is nothing in the world that could have stopped them running the Tourist Trophy race at Dundrod that year. And there is nothing in the world that would have stopped me from competing in the event now that I had a car, and one of the best at that. As I mentioned, it was my first drive in a big manufacturer's car and although I was not an official entry, they did co-opt me into the team. Things were made even more exciting for me because I was not to be twenty-one until the following day! I had never driven a car like this before and I am glad to say that I had never driven in conditions like that before, either. I drove as hard as I could and was lucky enough to pull away from the opposition and finally win the class, the race overall and be a member of the winning team. The following day, Bill

Lyons, as he was then, signed me up to lead the full works team the following year. What a way to come of age and what an introduction to a great marque!

From 16 September 1950 onwards, I drove all kinds of Jaguars in all kinds of races; from Monaco to the Mille Miglia. They were all great cars, some greater than others. Certainly they were best suited to smooth, high-speed tracks like Le Mans and Silverstone.

This book, which has been written by an enthusiast, for enthusiasts, is certainly a great tribute to those cars. Chris Harvey has obviously spent a tremendous amount of time researching and compiling his information. I cannot imagine that there are many questions that a reader would want to ask which will remain unanswered once he has read this interesting and well-illustrated book.

Stirling Moss O.B.E.

Acknowledgements
This book is the first of a series I had been mulling over in my mind for more than a year. I knew what I wanted in the book but I hadn't made up my mind exactly how it should be presented; I must thank Tim Parker, automotive editor of Osprey Publishing for pulling it all together and having such a profound effect on the final shape. I am deeply indebted also to Paul Skilleter for months of patient picture research, with Tim Parker again, Andrew Whyte, product liaison officer of Jaguar Cars, Warren Allport of *Autocar*, Jim Lee of *Motor*, John Dunbar of *Motor Sport*, Bob Smiley of the Empire Division of the Jaguar Clubs of North America, Heinz Schendzielorz of the Australian Jaguar clubs, and Tom March for the cover photography.

And for all those people who found pictures for Paul Skilleter and myself, there were so many more who helped with the words; all the people I've ever badgered for information about Jaguar competition cars over the years, such as Dave Preece, John Harper, Martin Crowther, Ruth Oldham, Wally Hassan, Roy Salvadori, Hugh Howorth, Jack Sears, Warren and Lawrence Pearce, Andrew Whyte, Clive Richardson and Denis Jenkinson of *Motor Sport*, Dave Cottingham, Ron Beaty, Roger Ludgate, Phil Porter, Ian Fraser of *CAR* magazine, Grant McMillan, Harvey Hingston, Dr Phillipe Renault, Ernie Foster, Barry Eccleston, Alan Hodge and Peter Taylor of British Leyland, Les Hughes (father and son), Simon Watney, Reg Woodcock, Dave Nursey, Jim Thomson, Graig Hinton, Carter Alexander, Ed Harrell, Peter and Sally Griffiths, Karl Heim, Ted Worswick, Paul Skilleter, and, of course, Stirling Moss.

I must also thank all the writers, anonymous and otherwise, whose publications listed in the bibliography have ensured that the wonderful story of the competition Jaguars will never be forgotten.

Photographic acknowledgements

The following persons and organizations kindly supplied photographs used in this book. They are listed alphabetically.

Autocar, p. 16 (top and bottom), 46, 49 (top), 50, 51, 54 (top and bottom), 55, 56, 57, 58 (top and bottom), 60, 64, 77, 78, 82, 84, 86 (top), 87 (top and bottom), 89 (top), 94, 96, 97 (top and bottom), 100, 102 (top), 105, 116, 126, 127, 136, 137, 138, 139 (top), 152, 158

Harold Barker, p. 148, 177

John E. Gaisford, p. 151

W.K. Henderson, p. 22

Jaguar Cars, p. 13 (top), 38 (bottom), 74, 199, 201

J.B. Kirton, p. 90

Leyland Cars, p. 27

London Art Technical, p. 183, 184, 185, 186, 187, 188, 189, 190, 191, 192, 194 (top), 196 (top and bottom), 197

Tom March, cover (front and back)

Karen Miller, p. 25

Motor, p. 10, 12, 13 (bottom), 14, 15 (bottom), 28, 30, 33, 34 (top and bottom), 36, 39, 40, 41 (top), 42, 48, 66, 70, 72, 73, 76, 83, 88 (top and bottom), 91 (bottom), 92, 95, 104, 106, 108, 110, 113, 114, 115 (top), 117 (top and bottom), 118, 123 (top), 128, 157, 160, 161 (top), 163 (bottom), 164, 166, 167, 170 (top and bottom), 172

Osborne Peacock and Co., p. 38 (top)

Planet News, p. 79

Lance J. Ruting, p. 120 (top)

Fred Scatley, p. 176

Heinz Schendzielorz, p. 115 (bottom)

Paul Skilleter, p. 19 (bottom), 20, 21, 23, 41 (bottom), 44, 45, 68 (top and bottom), 69, 98 (top and bottom), 99, 102 (bottom), 112, 119, 120 (bottom), 121, 122, 144, 149, 173 (bottom), 174, 178, 180, 182, 194 (bottom), 195

Sunrise Universal, p. 173 (top)

Temple Press, p. 132, 134, 140, 141, 142, 154, 156, 168, 169

Vachon, p. 80

Jack Harrop storms to a class win in the 1938 RAC Rally in his beautiful new Jaguar SS100, repeating his victory of the year before. The spectacular SS100 really was a bargain—it cost only £395 against the £695 of its perennial rival, the Frazer Nash BMW. Not only could it outperform the sophisticated German cars on faster courses, but it was the best-looking car of its day

Chapter 1
The car for all seasons

Historic racing is sweeping the competition world like wildfire. Glorious old racing cars that had been relegated to club racing in the nineteen-fifties and sixties are being revived everywhere to race at all the big meetings from Silverstone to Monterey. Enthusiasts used to attend grands prix purely to watch the greatest drivers pitting their skills against one another in the fastest cars the world had ever seen. Le Mans was still the greatest sports car race; people everywhere lined the roads to watch the Monte Carlo Rally. Then, spectator boredom set in. Today, all the competition cars look alike and their drivers can hardly be seen; they are buried in a mass of metal, plastic and life-support systems. This was evident by the late nineteen-sixties when spectators often spent more time reminiscing about the good old days than actually watching the racing. They wanted to see brave men and women driving cars, cars not far removed from those still used on the road, at breathtaking speed around race-tracks and over Alpine passes. In the wake of this wave of nostalgia came today's historic racing; the famous old competition cars were restored to their pristine glory and given races of their own. The promoters knew when they were on to a good thing. Now these races have become a major attraction, other series have been started, such as "Thoroughbred" racing for the cars that were far from exclusive in their day but have become rarities nowadays, and "Classic Saloon" car racing in the same vein. In all these fields, there were no greater cars than the Jaguars, from the SS100 to the Lister specials and lightweight E types; and it would be wrong to ignore the latter-day Jaguar racers, the XJ coupé and the XJ-S. They are all here in the chapters which follow. This chapter is to set the scene on what Jaguars were all about and to show why it is still such an emotive marque on the race-tracks today.

The story of the competition Jaguars is more than anything the story of one man, William Heynes, supported by others, such as William Lyons (later to become Sir

Peter Walker thrills the crowds watching the Silverstone Production Car Race in 1949. It was the competition debut of the Jaguar XK120 and the start of one of the longest careers in motor racing history; XK120 Roadsters are still winning races today! Walker finished second behind Leslie Johnson in another XK with the rest of the field trailing

William), who started the great dynasty in 1922; Harry Weslake, whose cylinder head work produced so much power; Wally Hassan, the development engineer forever associated with Brooklands specials; engine man Claude Baily; chassis expert Bob Knight; preparation chief Phil Weaver; aerodynamicist Malcolm Sayer; and test drivers such as Soapy Sutton and Norman Dewis.

But it was Heynes, who joined the company as chief engineer in 1935, who turned the superbly styled SS into a Jaguar supercar. With Weslake, he produced an overhead valve version of their current Standard engine; and motoring journalist Tommy Wisdom took off in the factory development car, BHW 77, or "Old Number Eight" as it was affectionately called from its chassis number. Wisdom and Sammy Newsome made good use of Heynes's new-found power for this famous Jaguar SS100, winning international rally awards and putting up astonishing times at Shelsley Walsh, the home of British hillclimbing, not to mention blazing round Brooklands. A Jaguar was already becoming something more than a pretty promenader.

The war that followed killed many a fine car, but helped produce an even better Jaguar. Heynes, Hassan, Lyons and Baily spent their spare time fire-watching at the company works in Foleshill, Coventry—and designing a new twin overhead camshaft engine when the Blitz had died down and bombs did not fall every night. Lyons also had an SS100 locked away at his home, Wappenbury Hall, and when the war was over this car was put to good use as Heynes and company developed a brand-new saloon to take their wonder engine.

left
Leslie Johnson hammers his factory XK120 Fixed-head coupé round the Montlhèry track in Paris in 1952 during one of the most dramatic record attempts ever. With Bert Hadley, Stirling Moss and Jack Fairman, he averaged 100.31 mph for seven days and nights, covering 16,851 miles and taking nine international records. The car was virtually standard except for a long-range fuel tank, C type engine options and a two-way radio. "Frequently, rude remarks could be heard coming over the air," said *Autosport*, "but the installation was invaluable in providing the pit personnel with the required information relating to oil pressure, engine temperature and so on . . ."

below
One of the most successful club racers of the early nineteen-fifties was Hugh Howorth in his self-prepared ex-Peter Walker XK120 Roadster. Here he fights fatigue to finish third in a Snetterton sports car race in April 1953 behind Cliff Davis's Tojeiro and Roy Salvadori's Frazer-Nash, following three sleepless nights rebuilding his engine

Jaguar C types raced everywhere in the early nineteen-fifties. In this picture, Stirling Moss in a works C type fresh from their victory at Le Mans the previous week leads Ian Stewart's Ecurie Ecosse C type and Hans Ruesch's 4.1-litre Ferrari in heat three of the British Empire Trophy race on the Isle of Man in 1953. Moss finished second in the heat and Ruesch third after Stewart retired with brake and clutch trouble. Reg Parnell won the heat in an Aston Martin DB3S more suited to the tight, bumpy circuit and went on to win the final with Moss fourth

The Lyons SS100 went to his future son-in-law, Ian Appleyard, Jaguar's distributor in Leeds, to replace one he had been using for rallies immediately after the war. This car, LNW 100, was to take Appleyard to a Coupé des Alpes in 1948 after an epic drive, and to win its class in the 1949 Tulip Rally. But by then it had already been made obsolete, although it covered Jaguar's name in glory. Lyons had decided that his new saloon car could do with a bit more publicity, so with Heynes he built a new sports car.

When the XK120 was launched in 1948 using the fire-watchers' engine, it took the sports car world by storm. Sutton averaged 132 mph with it at Jabbeke and the demand was such that Jaguars had to tool up for substantially more than the visualized production run of 200 or more. At the same time, they were preparing to launch the Mark VII saloon to replace the pre-war based Mark V and enthusiasts were competing with anything they could lay their hands on. Gordon Parker built a series of Jaguar-based specials,

Teamwork is essential in motor racing and never more so than at Le Mans. Here the Ecurie Belge C type of Laurant and de Tornaco receives attention in the pits on its way to ninth place behind the works cars in first, second and fourth places. As one mechanic refuels the car, another tops up the oil and a third cleans the screen under the watchful eyes of three scrutineers.

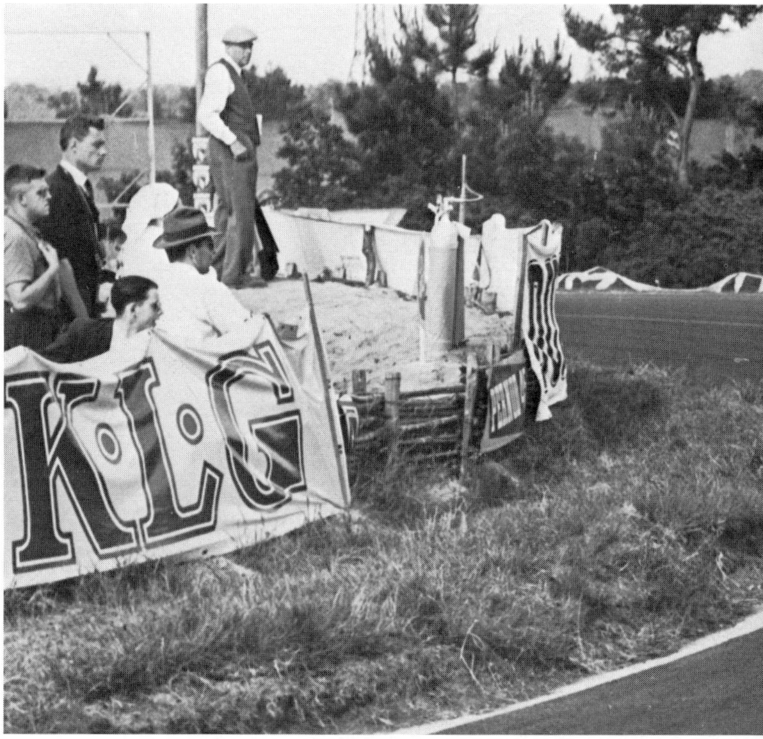

right
Mike Hawthorn overtakes Castellotti's 4.4-litre 121LM Ferrari for the lead at Le Mans in 1955. Hawthorn and Ivor Bueb went on to win a race marred by tragedy as more than eighty people died when a Mercedes crashed into the crowd. It was the D type's first victory at Le Mans after gaining second place in its debut in 1954. Castellotti retired with engine trouble

right
Ronnie Adams hurls his huge Mark VII Jaguar saloon sideways along a snow-packed Alpine road to win the Monte Carlo Rally in 1956. It was an extraordinary drive by the Ulsterman with his crew of Derek Johnston and Frank Biggar. And it was an extraordinary car, starring in one earlier Monte Carlo Rally and one Silverstone Production Car race. Despite its bulk, it vanquished all the smaller cars in both events, although no other car of more than 2500 cc finished in the first thirty-eight in the Monte!

below
There was no more patriotic team in motor racing than the Ecurie Ecosse. Here Ron Flockhart blazes through the night to win Le Mans 1957 with Bueb. It was the Scottish team's greatest victory and sadly marked the end of the D type's international long-distance racing career; they were never the same again when a change of regulations led to their 3.8-litre engines being replaced by 3-litre versions

The lightweight E types were the final embodiment of the works racing XK theme. This is the ex-Lumsden/Sargent car once registered 49 FXN, fitted with the ultimate Sayer-inspired low-drag bodywork. In this picture, John Carden fights off Robin Hamilton's Aston Martin DB4GT for fourth position in the *Classic Car* post-historic championship round at the Jaguar Drivers' Club spring meeting at Silverstone in 1974

starting with a Jaguette (MG chassis, SS engine), followed by a Jaguara (Buckler chassis, XK engine) and Frank Le Gallais anticipated all the trends with a rear-engined hillclimb special using Alec Issigonis's Citroën-based suspension and, first, a Mark V engine, then an XK. Strange as they might have seemed, these cars were race winners and so was Dubliner Cecil Vard in his stately Mark V saloon. He was the scourge of Monte Carlo Rallies, sweeping through the field into third and fifth places on two occasions in a car more suited to a duke or a dowager.

With these cars as back-up and brutal Allards as competition, there was nothing in the same class as the XK120 in the first Silverstone Production Car Race. They won as they wanted and Jaguars carried on winning this event right into the nineteen-sixties, with Mark VII saloons taking over when sports cars were channelled into separate events. The XK120, especially the Roadster, won countless events on race-tracks all over the world in the nineteen-fifties and dominated rally fields, with Appleyard adding to his collection of Coupés, until the advent of the Triumph TR.

The most successful Jaguar racing saloons were the Marks 1 and 2. Here John Sparrow drives the ex-works 3.8 Mark 2 in the Six-Hour Race at Brands Hatch in 1963, won by a similar car driven by Salvadori and world champion-to-be Denny Hulme

The most famous and most successful Jaguar special was the Lister, pictured here in its best-known form with "knobbly" body—the bare minimum of coachwork to cover the bulky mechanical components. The car, driven by long-time Jaguar exponent John Harper at Silverstone in 1973, is MVE 303, which was virtually unbeatable in Archie Scott-Brown's hands in the late nineteen-fifties. Even today the Lister-Jaguar is winning consistently in historic racing

Glorious reminder of a bygone era: Chris Stewart driving an ex-Phil Scragg cycle-winged HWM-Jaguar into fifth place in the historic sports car race at the Jaguar Drivers' Club Silverstone meeting in 1977. Bobby Bell and David Ham finished first and second in Lister-Jaguars, Rupert Glydon third in a Lola Mark 1, American Stephen Griswold fourth in Martin Morris's D type, OKV 3, and Stewart fifth

Mark VII saloons were also popular rally wagons, particularly in snow-bound events such as the Monte Carlo Rally, where their great weight and power enabled them to plough through the most severe drifts. The climax of their competition career came in 1956, when Ulsterman Ronnie Adams won the Monte in a works machine after repeated brilliant attempts.

As the Mark VII was putting up a good show on the race-track and in rallies, the XK120 was distinguishing itself, first at Le Mans, then in every form of national racing from British club events to SCCA racing, even in Far Eastern grands prix. It came agonizingly close to taking a place at Le Mans in 1950—so close that Lyons agreed to Heynes building a proper racing sports car based on the same components that would be more of a match for the specialized machinery the XK had been competing against. The brilliant C type (or XKC to use the chassis series definition), virtually conceived and built in six months, was more than a match for all the other sports racers. It won Le Mans—then the world's greatest sports car race—on its debut in 1951 and went on to win again in 1953 after pioneering the use of aircraft-style disc brakes. Heynes simply left all the other engineers trailing; and even then he was not content. In 1954 he came up with an even

Guy Beddington corners flat out in one of the fastest Jaguars ever raced, his modsports fuel injection V12 E type. Although spectacularly fast, this 500 bhp lightweight enjoyed little success: in the mid-nineteen-seventies nobody had made brakes capable of stopping it consistently! With more development it is potentially in a class of its own as a race-winner

Beautiful car, beautiful number: the great Scottish enthusiast Bob Kerr storms up the Rest and Be Thankful hill in his XK120 Fixed-head coupé in 1975

One of the current kings of the classic saloon car circuits is Bill Pinkney with his 2.4 Mark 1, pictured here at Silverstone in 1977. Bill's immaculate car is fitted with a 220 bhp big valve engine, but is otherwise substantially as standard

better design, the Sayer-inspired super-streamlined D type. The first D types were not called that—they were XKCs (for competition)—but they looked so different and so beautiful they deserved a name of their own; that is why they were christened D types by journalist Harold Hastings, and, for ever after, their chassis numbers were prefixed XKD. And what a debut the D types had! They fought a fearsome Ferrari for twenty-four hours at Le Mans and were only beaten by two miles! They were the darlings of the racegoers, even more so when they went on to win Le Mans three times in succession from 1955 to 1957, racing on there even until 1960. Without a doubt, the D type was one of the greatest, most graceful and most emotive cars ever made; many were the races it won and many were the races it might have won had it not been designed, like the C type, purely to win at Le Mans.

It was on the tighter, rougher, courses that its Achilles' heel was exposed; its rear suspension was only at its best on a billiard table. But what a wonderful engine it used, the ultimate XK of the nineteen-fifties producing more than 300 bhp and, like everything Jaguar, an absolute bargain in terms of cost. No wonder myriad special builders, starting with HWM at Walton-on-Thames, turned out so many ultra-lightweight circuit racers to accept this magnificent power unit. These highly specialized cars simply mopped-

Two of the ill-fated works XJCs, driven by Schenken and Rouse, lead the eventual race-winner, Dieter Quester's BMW, in the 1977 Tourist Trophy. Schenken, in the dry sump Jaguar lasted thirty-six laps before losing a wheel; Rouse in the wet sump car disputed the lead until he lost the car on a patch of oil with less than ten laps to go. But while the Big Cats were on the track they doubled crowd attendances, such was their awe-inspiring performance

up races everywhere with Sir William Lyons's connivance: he was happy to see a Jaguar-engined device beating the rival Aston Martins, Ferraris and Maseratis any day.

Soon HWM were joined by Cooper, Tojeiro, then Lister. The Tojeiro-Jaguar was the lightest and fastest of the lot, but was difficult to handle and enjoyed little success; not so the Lister-Jaguar, particularly in the hands of the legendary Archie Scott-Brown. He raced all his days with handicaps that would have defeated a lesser man, making up for a malformed hand and feet with an extraordinary sense of balance. Until a tragic accident, there was hardly anybody who could stay with Scott-Brown and his Lister-Jaguar; Walt Hansgen, too, in a similar car, was as well-nigh invincible in the States.

Until sports racing car regulations were changed, Jaguars were simply the greatest with their classic 3.8 engines. When the maximum displacement was reduced to 3 litres in 1958 they were in trouble—the Foleshill Fire-watchers' six never raced well below 3.4 litres. But at 3.4 litres, then 3.8 litres, it dominated saloon car racing with the Mark 1 and Mark 2 saloons from 1957 to 1963; as ever

below
Even today, there's still a Jaguar XK racing in SCCA events—and, what's more, it's still winning against much more modern machinery! Here Bob Smiley beats a Jensen-Healey, Triumph TR250 and a TVR at Bridgehampton in August 1978 with his immaculate XK140. Bridgehampton was the Long Island circuit where Walt Hansgen scored numerous wins in Briggs Cunningham's D type twenty years ago. Smiley's times are faster—showing how far the XK140 and modern racing tyres have developed

there was simply nothing in the same class as these cars beloved by racing drivers, rallymen, business executives and bank robbers. It took 7 litres of Detroit iron to defeat them in 1963, and by then the E type sports car, based on the D type, had been launched with sophisticated independent rear suspension, in 1961. Lightweight examples of these cars so nearly took international racing by storm until tyres grew wider and wider in 1964 and sports cars ceased to bear much resemblance to anything that could be used on the road. Still the E type raced on, to mop up production sports car racing, then modsports, when they were joined by a fantastic plastic-bodied XK120 that took lap records everywhere when driven by John Pearson. But that was 1970, and by then the Lister-Jaguar and other specials were starting to dominate historic racing with rejuvenated D types. So Jaguar entered the nineteen-seventies with a potential race-winner somewhere every weekend; they had abandoned work on a twelve-cylinder successor to the D type in 1967 in the face of spiralling costs. But the single overhead camshaft 5.3-litre unit developed by Heynes from this car's engine was to power the last of the E types, which

The most successful Jaguar racing since 1975 has been WPU 207, the fearsome XK120 Roadster entered by Oldham and Crowther for David Preece, seen here leading a Lotus Elan in modsports at Brands Hatch in 1978. In forty-seven races between October 1975 and July 1978 it broke eleven lap records and took pole position twenty times, winning the Thoroughbred Championship in 1976, 1977 and 1978. During the 1978 season it was also raced in the modsports championship, the conversion to wide wheels, low profile tyres, full width windscreen and change of rear axle taking twelve hours between events!

won the first British production sports car championship in the nineteen-seventies, then SCCA titles in America just as the last E types were being sold in 1975.

It was then that Jaguars threw caution to the winds and invested a vast sum in V12 racing coupés for the European Touring Car Championship—shades of the Silverstone sales-spinners all over again. These XJ coupés were wonderful machines, the nearest Britain has had to a national racing team since BRM in the nineteen-fifties. But the red, white and blue giants were none too reliable, just as the BRM had been, and they faded away after little more than a season of wild excitement; a season that had promised so much, such was the potential spectacle of these incredibly fast cars.

But all was not lost: Group 44's XJ-S twelve-cylinder coupé rose like a phoenix from the flames of taxpayers' wrath which engulfed the ill-fated XJ coupé project, to carry all before it in TransAm racing. Once more a Jaguar was on the winning trail with nothing else to match it, as all their historic racers continued to thrill crowds everywhere, just as they had done in their heyday.

Yet another spectacular success story: Bob Tullius takes his Group 44 XJ-S coupé to the SCCA TransAm championship in 1978. He clinched the Category One title—his second successive in the XJ-S—at Road Atlanta in September with his fifth win in a row. Hard on his tail is a rival Porsche, which, apart from a variety of Corvettes, was the only car in the same league as the Jaguar

Not strictly Jaguar, but their SS ancestors: Lyons's first real works team of S.S.1 tourers for the 1933 International Alpine Trial. From the right, Humfrey Symons (number eighteen), Charles Needham (number nineteen), Miss Margaret Allen (number twenty) and Austrian SS distributor Georg Hans Koch, who entered number thirty-eight privately. He finished sixth in class ahead of the only surviving works car, driven by Needham to eighth place. The factory had increased their cars' compression ratio substantially just before the event with the result that they suffered from chronic overheating. Nevertheless, Koch's performance was considered to be quite good as the only cars which finished in front of him in his class were five fabulously expensive Bugattis

Chapter 2
SS is for supersports

It stood there long and lithe, wire wheels a-glistening, radiator standing proud between the dumb-irons. Two great headlights were gleaming in the sun, windscreen folded flat, doors cut away, spare wheel mounted on a great slab tank. And more than anything, what wonderful wings . . . they swept up from the front like the wings of a bat, and all along the sides like an ocean wave, and over the back with a hint of a pagoda curve; it was a brand-new Jaguar. "Coo! Look—a racer," gasped the small boy. It was 1936 and the Wisdoms had just collected their SS100, chassis number 18008, from Foleshill. It was a completely standard $2\frac{1}{2}$ litre, but for years after hearing that little boy's exclamation, Wisdom called it "my racer".

"Racer or not, it certainly could move," he told his avid audience in *Jaguar Journal* ten years later. "It was after my wife and I had carried out extended road trials on it that we conceived the idea of driving it in the International Alpine Trial, although well aware that, if we did so, we would be up against formidable opposition. . . .

"To say that we started the Trial light-heartedly and with no greater hope than that of putting up a good show would be a fairly accurate description of our feelings when we took our place with the seventy-odd competitors at Lucerne. By the finish of that first day's punishing drive to Lugano I had added to an already wholesome respect for the capabilities of the Jaguar." And by the end of the rally—acknowledged as one of the toughest in the world—everybody had a far greater respect for the capabilities of the SS100. It put up the fastest time in its class, the over 2000 cc, in all four speed trials and lost no marks on the road; as a result the Wisdoms won one of the few International Glacier Cups—the pre-war equivalent of a Coupé des Alpes—and first in their class. The Wisdoms had won the rally and everybody knew it. The SS100 was no longer a "cad's car", all show and no performance; it was a real sports car.

Now Wisdom had only been borrowing BHW 77; it was the works development car and as soon as it returned from

The first real competition appearance of a Jaguar sports car: the Hon. Brian Lewis storms Shelsley Walsh in his SS Jaguar 90 in 1935. He recorded fifty-two seconds to finish third in class, one second behind the winner, A. Powys-Lybbe's Alvis

62
ARW 395

George Abecassis in an SS Car Club driving test at Foleshill in the mid-nineteen-thirties in his extraordinary SS100 special complete with faired-in dumb-irons and Brooklands exhaust. Needless to say this fast, if somewhat accident-prone, driver used his car to great effect

Trials were of paramount importance to motor manufacturers in the nineteen-thirties and something of a national sport, rather akin to rallying today. Despite their great power and relatively narrow wheels, the SS100s competed against far more specialized Allards, MGs and Austins. Note the twin rear wheels carried by H. Bolton in the 1937 London to Edinburgh Trial: this was a popular feature of trials cars, increasing the weight over the rear axle. Usually these were the normal back wheels used on the road, knobbly-tyred trials wheels having been substituted before the timed off-road hillclimbs. This arrangement suited the SS100 well, as it was inclined to consume tyres when driven with spirit

the Alpine Trial it was stripped, checked and handed over to Sammy Newsome to drive at Shelsley Walsh. There could not have been much wrong with it; it spent no more than a few days at the factory before Newsome won the over 3000 cc class in the September meeting at the home of British hillclimbing in 51.62 seconds, a second faster than the Hon. Brian Lewis is his SS90. Probably the only real modification had been the fitting of a higher-compression cylinder head.

Meanwhile Wisdom was itching to get his hands back on "his racer"—or Old Number Eight as BHW was becoming known after its number plate was deemed to be superfluous for track work. A few other things were superfluous, too. It lost its wings, screen, lamps and other odds and ends, enough to help it lap the Outer Circuit at Brooklands in October at 104.41 mph in Wisdom's hands to finish second behind the supercharged Appleton Special and in front of another highly tuned racing car, the Alta of George Abecassis.

Old Number Eight was not the only SS competing in those heady pre-war years. Old Number Seven won the 2000–3000 cc class in the Marne sports car grand prix at Rheims in 1936 for Australian F. J. McEvoy, and stable-mates had been picking up awards in rallies and races since 1932; but Old Number Eight was the first of the Jaguars to cover the Coventry firm in glory.

right
The works cars ready to start the RAC Rally in 1937. Number 143 was driven by Lewis and Davis and number 144 by Jaguar publicist Ernie Rankin and Jacob. With the Wisdoms in BHW 77, they won the much-prized manufacturer's team award besides individual trophies

below
The factory team of SS100s entered the RAC Rally again in 1938—but suffered at the hands of their close rivals, the BMW 328s. In many ways they were at a disadvantage against the expensive German thoroughbreds, such was their relative bulk when compared to the nimble BMW. The 3½-litre Jaguars had little difficulty winning the final speed tests, though

Wisdom won more rally awards in 1937 with BHW 77 back in standard trim, before she was again stripped and a prototype $3\frac{1}{2}$-litre engine fitted. In Newsome's hands, it stormed Shelsley in 45·52 seconds to everybody's astonishment. And in Wisdom's hands it caught the handicapper hopping, to win at 111.85 mph in the Brooklands October meeting. It looked outwardly normal, said one observer, the renowned Bill Boddy, who used to occupy an office at the track in Weybridge, putting together *Brooklands—Track and Air* before becoming editor of *Motor Sport* and doyen of British motoring journalists. But it won comfortably by 12 seconds from H. J. Aldington's BMW and Oats in a 12/50 Alvis. Old Number Eight was said to be standard except for magneto ignition, and a compression ratio of 11:1 rather than its rally-winning 7:1.

Those were the days when compression ratios went up and up, hoping that the handicapper would not notice, until the car won something. It seems doubtful that handicapper Ebblewhite ever forgave Wisdom!

As development continued apace on Old Number Eight with more than 150 bhp being extracted on methanol-based fuel, standard $3\frac{1}{2}$-litre SS100s were wiping up rally awards. Jack Harrop won his class in the RAC Rally of 1938 and Mrs V. E. M. Heatherington won her class in the Welsh Rally. At Shelsley, Newsome got down to 43.6 seconds despite gearbox trouble, reducing this to 42.95 seconds in June 1939, just before war broke out. In this form, Old Number Eight had a 14:1 compression ratio and won the $3\frac{1}{2}$-litre unsupercharged class with only a couple of supercharged racers, Baron's 3.3-litre Bugatti and Ruesch's 3.8-litre Alfa, in front. Wisdom practised the car at Brooklands at 125 mph before the crankshaft broke and war was declared.

The factory kept Old Number Eight throughout the war, and Wisdom's wife, Elsie, used it to win the ladies' class in the Bouley Bay hillclimb in 1947. But, as Lyons and company concentrated on developing the XK engine and

One of the most successful SS circuit racers was a $2\frac{1}{2}$-litre 100 driven by C. E. Truett. In much-modified form it was substantially faster than average and even quicker than many $3\frac{1}{2}$-litres. Here it battles with a BMW 328 at Crystal Palace with Abecassis's white SS100 hard on their heels

the Mark V saloon's new torsion bar independent front suspension, work on sports cars took a back seat. Enthusiasts, accordingly, had to make do with their pre-war 100s for what sport there was—chiefly sprints and hillclimbs because petrol was so scarce. These drivers included Jaguar's Yorkshire distributor, Ian Appleyard, who drove a 1938 SS100 in the first post-war Alpine, held in 1947.

Appleyard was a great rally man, especially good at the driving tests that sorted out the top contestants when the field reached its ultimate destination in, say, Cannes or Nice. But tyres were scarcer than hen's teeth in the Europe of 1947 and the SS100 certainly had an appetite for them. Punctures, blow outs and bald treads consigned Appleyard to third in class. Nevertheless, he was determined to have another go at the rally the following year and had the luck to acquire a unique SS100; although, doubtless, Lyons was well aware of his talent.

right
The S.S. Car Club organized a full programme before the war, with something for everybody. A popular weekend's sport would be a night out at the White Hart Hotel in Salisbury, followed by a rally over the hills to the Branksome Tower Hotel in Bournemouth, where the President's Trophy was presented at a dinner dance. Here's the muddy part: E. E. Howe's SS100 plunges down a rough lane near Wilton on the road to Bournemouth with Truett hard on his heels—a far cry from circuit racing. Sadly, somebody made off with the S.S. Car Club's funds after one of these pleasant events and the patron, Lyons, regarded initial attempts to set up the Jaguar Drivers' Club in 1955 with some suspicion

right
S.S. Cars proudly show off their Old Number Eight in full hillclimbing trim before the war. The twin rear wheels were for better traction, of course, and the back axle had been moved forward four inches with new springs on the lightened chassis to shorten the wheelbase. The detachable tail was much abbreviated and contained one of a variety of fuel tanks, with sizes to suit individual events. But most of the development centred on the engine, which yielded nearly 170 bhp in its most highly tuned form—around 50 bhp more than a standard SS100

This car was one of the last $2\frac{1}{2}$-litres to come off the production lines as the factory went over to war work in 1940. It was then stored at the Lyons home, Wappenbury Hall, Warwickshire, until 1947, when it was returned to the factory to be rebuilt with a $3\frac{1}{2}$-litre engine. Subsequently it was given to Appleyard, who registered it LNW 100, with delivery mileage only on the clock.

"Apart from its having done a very low mileage, the car was identical with any other $3\frac{1}{2}$-litre Jaguar 100 in the country, but with vivid recollections of tattered tyres in last year's event, I did make provision for carrying a second spare wheel this time and managed to secure a great improvement in steering lock by a bit of judicious filing and bending at the front end," Appleyard reported in *Jaguar Journal* in 1948. Such were the modifications deemed necessary to compete in a top international rally immediately after the war!

Appleyard and his navigator, Dr Dick Weatherhead, even found time to compete for an unofficial Aix-les-Bains hillclimb cup during the initial stages of the rally! So far as these first road stages were concerned the biggest peril seemed to be three compulsory cocktail parties in Marseilles.

Hours later seventy cars with drivers from eight countries were lined up for the start at 11 pm: Delahaye, Hotchkiss, Citroën, Renault and Simca from France; Allard, Jaguar, Healey, Sunbeam-Talbot and HRG from Britain; Lancia from Italy. The route took them to Aix-les-Bains and the

Preparing to start the Alpine Trial from the Old Port at Marseilles in July 1948. Alongside Appleyard's SS100 is Alexander Black's Bentley Mark VI, later to demolish a roadside post and break a rear spring during hectic cornering in the Alps. Note the Bentley's oversize driving lamp, part of the sumptuous equipment on this stately rally car

The $2\frac{1}{2}$-litre Jaguar SS special which won the first race to be held at Goodwood after the war—a three-lap scratch event organized by the Junior Car Club in September 1948. "Goodwood is the best thing to have happened to British motor racing since the war," said *Motor Sport*, reporting on the great win by P. C. de F. C. Pycroft, a pre-war SS driver in his "weird" new aerodynamic coupé. It had a fan tail as part of the roof, and led throughout the race to win at 66.42 mph from two Healeys—with Pycroft holding down the top! No doubt it continued to give trouble as it was photographed here with no sign of a roof. It was also significant in that it bore a marked resemblance to the XK120 to come

unofficial night cup, which Appleyard might have won had he not made a mistake with the stopwatch and arrived at the top too early, followed by a run to Lugano and then to Chamonix for the real terror: a four-hundred-mile race to Nice taking in five successive passes of more than 7000 feet, distinguished by hairpins and perilous drops with surfaces like a tank testing track.

"The tolerance at controls had been reduced to only one minute late or early," said Appleyard, "and in addition an entirely new penalty-earning device had been incorporated. Somewhere on the 1200-mile route (from Marseilles) would be two unannounced timed hillclimbs. These might be anywhere and one's only warning of entry into a timed section would be a man waving a French flag and a blackboard chalked with a figure showing the length in kilometres of the climb. A very high target speed was set for each class and penalty points would be awarded for non-attainment. If nobody in a class reached the set average, then anybody taking more than five per cent longer than the best man in the class would be penalised one point per fifth of a second late.

"This seemed a very tough proposition as it meant that although one might complete the entire trial without being late at any control, a bit of bad luck in getting baulked by a lorry or bus in a timed climb could ruin one's entire chances."

Refuelling on the move, with Weatherhead perched precariously on the tail pouring petrol into that great slab

left
The SS100 continued to put up a good show long after it was obsolete. Here R. N. Lee swings into a box during the Bolton-le-Moors Car Club's Rally Driving Tests in March 1952. The event, held near Chorley, Lancs., attracted a star-studded field of more than 150, with the Mayor of Bolton presiding over the post-rally dinner and presentations. "Best performance of the day was put up by the crafty master of special tests, Ken Bailey in his Vauxhall-powered special," reported *Autosport*. Appleyard finished third in his XK120

below left
Tommy Wisdom hits the nostalgia trail in Old Number Eight at the Jaguar Drivers' Club XK Day in 1971. Pre-war SS100 competitor George Matthews bought Old Number Eight from the factory in 1948, before crashing it at Boreham and selling it to dealer Harry Webb, who passed it on to A. H. Mecrow. He fitted it with rudimentary wings and lights and re-registered it for roadwork as KDG 20 in 1951. The next owner was A. E. Guy, who converted its engine to more standard specification and drove it at Prescott and Oulton Park. Soon after it disappeared and did not reappear again until it was discovered in poor condition in Liverpool in 1968. It then passed into the hands of restorer David Barber, who returned it to its old glory—for Wisdom to drive again

The SS100 in its element, storming an Alpine pass on which its sheer power could be used to its greatest advantage. Appleyard had a relatively well-ordered run until he was delayed for ten minutes in a queue for petrol and spent another twenty-five minutes by the roadside so that his navigator, Dr Dick Weatherhead, could attend to an injured driver—the result was a hell-for-leather dash to the finish, and a victory that would have been missed if they had taken a second longer

14
LNW 100

Barber spent a lot of time developing Old Number Eight for historic racing in the early nineteen-seventies. Here he competes at Silverstone with a special $3\frac{1}{2}$-litre engine using original lozenged pistons and experimental pre-war factory cylinder head. With further development it was to beat an ERA in a straight fight!

tank, Appleyard passed numerous cars that had crashed, including an HRG that had gone over a banking and a Bentley that had demolished a post—neither with serious injury to their occupants. But they couldn't carry on when they came across Norman Hiskin's Sunbeam-Talbot, which had plunged into a ravine. The passenger, called Marsden, had been flung out and was badly hurt. Hiskin was still in the car and had only been saved from being crushed to death because the car had become lodged, like a bridge, over a stream at the bottom of the ravine. "Mr Appleyard and his passenger, Dr Weatherhead, sacrificed valuable time in rendering first aid to the injured Marsden," said the official report. What actually happened was that Appleyard and Weatherhead stopped so long that it seemed impossible for them to complete the first stage in time. The hectic drive that followed was related in Jaguar's house journal in 1949:

"For some miles I drove at a snail's pace—reaction after seeing the crash, I suppose. Then gradually the queer feeling wore off and soon we were dicing as never before. But the road gave us no chance to get up speed. Twisting incessantly it wound up and down over scrub-covered hills towards the coast. Not until Grasse did it begin to straighten out at all, but it was almost too late. We had exactly half an hour left for the thirty-two miles to the finish—that meant averaging sixty-four mph all the way into Cannes and along through Juan towards Nice on roads which were seething

with Saturday afternoon holidaymakers. It was a terrifying ride. Clocking between seventy and eighty mph most of the way, and with horn blaring incessantly, we passed obstructive vehicles on whichever side looked the more promising, whilst cyclists scattered before us like chaff in a hurricane. Cars coming against us were often forced on to the pavement as we swerved in and out of the traffic stream, whilst all around us sounded the horns of dozens of outraged Frenchmen. But as we emerged on to the promenade at Nice there was still a minute to go and with the speedo needle creeping towards the century mark, the Jaguar hurtled towards the final control. Dick was ticking off the seconds now. We'd just do it if nobody got in the way. Those final few yards seemed to take ages as we screeched to a standstill and handed over our route card. It was stamped. We were in on time."

Appleyard won four trophies, including a Glacier Cup, and was acclaimed the outright winner of the XIth International Alpine Trial; Jaguars were still a force to be reckoned with and the SS100 continued to win awards in rallies years after it had been made obsolete by the war. Today, they are a rare sight in competition with only Old Number Eight making effective forays into historic racing (to the detriment of pure racing machines such as ERAs), although the great French collector Dr Phillipe Renault is prone to air his three occasionally. Now they really are historic, setting the scene for even greater Jaguars to come.

Old Number Eight in action again. In 1974, it was supercharged for even better performance, eventually circulating only a little slower than Patrick Lindsey's ultra-competitive 250F Maserati in 1975!

One of the greatest moments in Jaguar's history as Ron "Soapy" Sutton crosses the measured mile line flat out at 132.596 mph in the second prototype XK120, chassis number 670002. The car, later converted to right-hand drive and registered HKV 500, behaved impeccably throughout. The only component which seemed to have had unfair demands made on it was the 120 mph speedometer!

Chapter 3
The excellent XKs

There have been some very great days in Jaguar's history. But there is one date that nobody in Coventry should ever forget: 22 October, 1948, when they wheeled out one of the greatest cars the world has ever seen. Bill Lyons and the famous four fire-watchers visualized it only as an appetizer for the big saloons to come. But the XK120 was such a glorious combination of performance and panache, and a bargain to boot, that it became one of the company's greatest products; and one of the greatest competition cars of all time. For thirty years it has been the car to beat in one event or another: in record runs, production car races, international rallying, club events, modsports and thoroughbred racing in that order; and few other cars have been able to live with it.

The Jaguar XK's debut was sensational, to put it mildly. Not only did it look good, but Lyons reckoned that the 120 stood for miles per hour—twice the maximum of most cars so many years ago—and it cost only £998 (about a quarter the price of a V12 Ferrari, which was the only car in the same league).

Needless to say, there were a lot of sceptics. But Jaguars, full of the bulldog spirit, decided to teach them a lesson. They told test driver Soapy Sutton, a figure straight from *Biggles*, to pack up his old kitbag and head for Belgium with one of the prototypes. Meanwhile Jaguar's top brass flew over a junket of journalists in the latest Dakota, and Soapy, fortified by numerous cups of tea, zoomed down the Jabbeke motor road, hood and screen erect, at no less than 126.448 mph; 132.596 mph with aero screen and undershield.

The world was agog but still wondering how such a bolide would figure on the track. Their answer came when three XKs, patriotically painted in red, white and blue, lined up for Britain's first production car race at Silverstone in August 1949. Leslie Johnson and Peter Walker left all the Allards, Healeys and Nashes trailing. What's more, they did it in style—they didn't even take off their rear spats!

Far right
Veteran Bert Hadley laps like clockwork in the leading works XK120 at Le Mans in 1950. At one point the car, shared with Leslie Johnson, rose to second place, but after twenty-one hours' racing it was retired with the clutch burned out. But the retirement was no disappointment: it was the dawning of the glory years for Jaguar . . .

Their preparation for Le Mans was a shade more serious in 1950. They abandoned both spats and bumpers, fitted high compression pistons (9:1) and proceeded to circulate like clocks until Johnson's leading XK had to retire while holding third place. It had cooked its brakes and Johnson eventually burned out his clutch by using that for all his braking. Disappointing? Not on your life. These were virtually standard cars and the rest were mostly racers. Chief engineer Mungo Heynes said he was sure that they could win next year if he could build some special cars based on standard components. His boss, Lyons, agreed. It was the dawning of the glory years, the years in which the name of Jaguar swept the world, gaining an unparalleled reputation for speed, quality and style. Heynes's extra-special XKs, the C type and the D type, went on to win at Le Mans in 1951, 1953, 1955, 1956 and 1957 and were still competitive until 1960!

Motoring correspondent Tommy Wisdom presses on to report the 1950 Silverstone Production Car Race for the *Daily Herald* from the hot seat of his semi-works XK120. Hard on his heels is French grand prix star Raymond Sommer in the leading works Aston Martin DB2 and Sydney Allard in his Ardun-Allard. Peter Walker won the race in a similar car to Wisdom's with Tony Rolt second in another XK120. Duncan Hamilton was third in a Healey Silverstone, Sommer fourth and Allard fifth. Wisdom almost had time to write his introduction as he came in thirteenth

17

24
JWK 988

Lord Louth wins the over 2-litre sports car class at the Bouley Bay hillclimb in July 1952 in 64.4 seconds. It was the fastest sports car time on the course in Jersey, with Ken Wharton setting fastest time of the day with 55.4 seconds in his 1000 cc supercharged Cooper. Long-time Jaguar exponent Bertie Bradnack took the 1000 cc to 2000 cc racing car class with 61.2 seconds in his unsupercharged 1100 cc Cooper with Frank Le Gallais winning the over 2-litre racing car class with his XK120-engined LGS in 56.2 seconds

Meanwhile the privateers were modifying their XK120 Roadsters. Deep in California, postmaster's son Philip T. Hill Jr was clenching his teeth and boring out his XK to 3.8 litres in company with one John Fitch. It was the very limit to which you could stretch the 3.4-litre block, but they did it and went on to win everything going on the West Coast. Hill (eventually to become world champion in 1961) was only one of the great drivers who started their careers on XKs. Hill and company were also among the first to fit Borrani alloy-rimmed wire wheels and Alfin steel-lined alloy drums to help cool the XK's overworked brakes. All this brake fade was a new problem. The XK was one of the first production sports cars to have small steel wheels (sixteen inches!) enclosed in an all-enveloping body. Before, it had been a case of big wheels (nineteen inches or more) rolling out in the airstream. These big wheels, running in flimsy cycle-type wings, allowed the use of huge exposed drums, which minimized brake fade. The XK's all-enveloping body gave it a much higher top speed, but effectively shrouded the brakes, which were, in any case,

limited in diameter by the small wheels. And nobody in Britain would make wire wheels in the new sizes at a reasonable price until Donald Healey persuaded Dunlops to produce them for his new 100 four-cylinder by offering them a ten-year contract, in 1952. So it was a case of fitting Borranis if you could get them through import controls and afford them—these Italian wonder-wheels, so beloved of Enzo Ferrari, cost £60 each in war-blighted Britain, roughly a quarter of the list price of the complete car!

Johnson's XK, along with five other thinly disguised works machines, eventually got wire wheels and promptly started to win all manner of events. And Lyons's son-in-law, Ian Appleyard, stormed to a succession of Coupés des Alpes (wins in any other language) in the Alpine Rally with the immortal NUB 120, and for the next three or four years as many as one-third of the competitors in any rally of importance drove XK120 Roadsters.

There was only one other car that had that sort of dominance in competition in 1950: the Cooper 500, a sort of prehistoric, bug-like Formula Ford powered by a motor-

Invincible driver, invincible car: Ian Appleyard at the height of his career in the famous semi-works XK120, NUB 120. Appleyard's speciality was the driving tests which sorted out the general classification at the end of rallies in the immediate post-war years. Here he rounds a pylon on the promenade at Morecambe, Lancs., to win the British seaside resort's rally in 1951. It was no minor event: the entry list was nearly as long and formidable as that of the RAC Rally

During the spring of 1953, Appleyard and Jaguars pensioned off NUB 120 at 100,000 miles and replaced it with another 120 Roadster, RUB 120. Appleyard is pictured here winning the over 2600 cc class in the Alpine Rally in July 1953 after putting up fastest time on the fantastic climb of the Stelvio Pass and another fastest for the standing kilometre at Monza. Later, in 1954, RUB 120 was rebodied as a Drop-head coupé to compete as a four-seater

cycle engine. They raced like locusts and their star driver was a good-looking youngster called Stirling Moss. His father had money and he could drive, but that wasn't enough in those days. "You must have experience," all the big manufacturers told the eager young man. Then journalist Tommy Wisdom, who had been racing a semi-works XK, opted to drive an official works-entered Jowett Jupiter in Britain's most glamorous sports car race, the Tourist Trophy. That left one of the top six XKs free . . . and Wisdom, who always had an eye for talent, offered the wheel to Moss. Enthusiasts who couldn't make it to Ulster saved their petrol ration and huddled round their radio sets to hear the familiar tale on the first lap of the three-hour event: Johnson's white XK was in the lead. Their handlebar moustaches twitched when the news came through that a green XK driven by Moss was lying second on the notoriously treacherous rain-soaked course. "Just a flash in the pan, Algy," they said, "he'll never last." That's true, he couldn't hold second place because by the second lap he had overtaken the maestro, Johnson. After that, it was Moss all the way to Jaguar's first post-war long-distance victory. He covered a total of 225.45 miles at 75.15 mph in dreadful conditions at Dundrod. And there was more than one reason to celebrate: the day after was Moss's twenty-first birthday. Jaguars and Moss, who was signed on the spot, had really come of age.

Ancient and modern. Stirling Moss in Tommy Wisdom's XK120 storms past John Buncombe's beam-axled HRG in the 1950 Tourist Trophy at Dundrod. Moss went on to record a historic win in the race and to take the top class with Buncombe finishing fourth in the class for smallest cars as the first HRG behind three of the new independent front suspension works MG TDs

above
John Swift was not only one of the fastest British Jaguar drivers in the early nineteen-fifties but one of the smartest in appearance. Here he presses hard for the lead in the 1952 British Empire Trophy race in his immaculate and highly modified XK120 while attired in a neat collar and tie and double-breasted jacket. Eventually the Swift roadster succumbed to a burned-out clutch; Sir James Scott-Douglas of the Ecurie Ecosse was best-placed Jaguar driver in sixth position behind winner Pat Griffith in a Lester-MG

right
Joint favourite Hugh Howorth—quoted at evens with Duncan Hamilton—streaks into the lead in the William Lyons Trophy race for XK120s at Boreham, Essex, in 1951. However, Howorth was so hard-pressed in his ex-Peter Walker roadster JWK 977 (chassis 660042) that he spun at Gilhooley and let Hamilton through to win. As Howorth fought to extract an oil drum course marker from under his chassis, Swift streaked past into second place and Roy Salvadori took third

The same sort of story was re-enacted throughout the world: drivers who had cut their teeth on spindly MG TCs hit the big time with XKs; drivers such as the Texan pig farmer Carroll Shelby, who was to win Le Mans with Roy Salvadori for Aston Martin in 1959 and went on to create the fearsome AC Cobra. Drivers such as Duncan Hamilton, who threw his XK around like he flew a Spitfire in a dogfight. Drivers such as the Belgian hard-men, Johnny Claes and Jacques Ickx (the grand prix star's father), who won the Liège-Rome-Liège Rally—in reality the world's roughest road race—in an XK. Drivers such as Sir James Scott-Douglas, as big as a baronial hall, who helped get the glorious Scottish Ecurie Ecosse off the ground with XK120s. They were the famous names, but there is one long forgotten, who was even faster on his day: Hugh Howorth, king of the club racers.

He had taken over Peter Whitehead's old semi-works XK, JWK 977, painted it black and silver, and made it go even faster. With Hill in America he was one of the first to take the risk of boring out the block to 3814 cc (Jaguars

Salvadori, fresh from an accident at Silverstone, shows he has lost none of his flair in the Lyons Trophy Race at Boreham. Here he hurls the XK round the rain-soaked airfield perimeter track that has since become a Ford testing ground, in one of his all-too-rare appearances in a Jaguar before signing for the rival Aston Martin works team

96
96
LOE 353

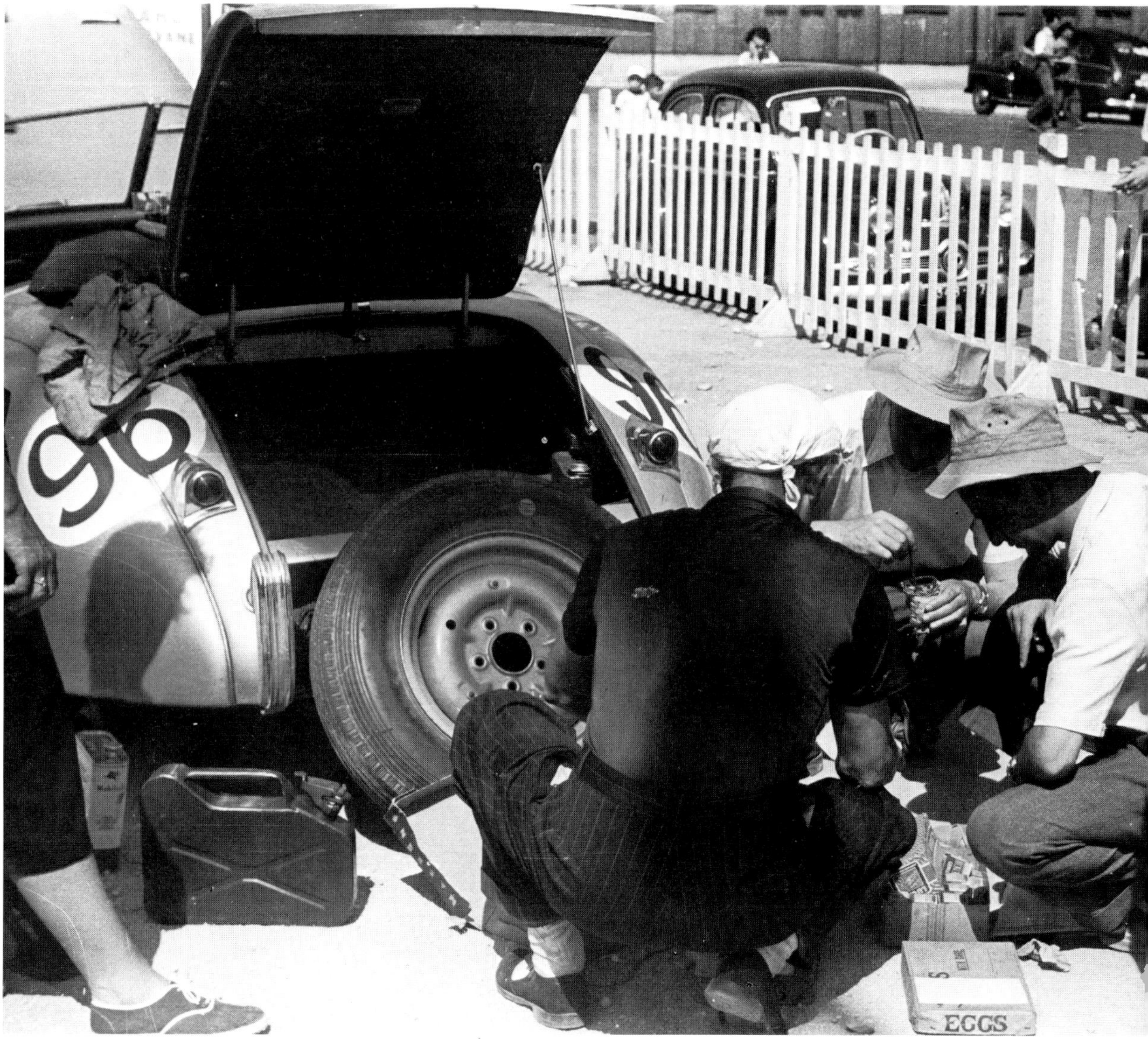

Almost inevitably, the Appleyards won a Coupe des Alpes in the 1951 Alpine Rally and took first place in the premier over 3-litre class, fractionally ahead of Imhof and Robertson's Cadillac-Allard with Swiss privateers Habitsreutinger and Horning third in another XK. They all secured Coupes des Alpes for penalty-free runs and Soler in fourth place helped Jaguar scoop the team award. But it was not all joy for the Jaguars. Speeds not far short of those seen on the race tracks had to be maintained over 2000 miles of potholes, hairpins and perilous mountain passes, and through torrential rain, fog and scorching sun, not to mention the cloying clouds of dust, as Sutcliffe demonstrates in his 120 Roadster on the descent of the Falzarego Pass. It was not surprising, therefore, that somebody, such as Sutcliffe, had to lose time with a leaking fuel tank as the second picture, taken at Marseilles, shows. It was then just a case of patching it up with spares carried in the boot; the days of works service teams were a long way off

MILLE MIGLIA
COPPA FRANCO MAZZOTTI
PIRELLI
Castrol
614
TI·11869

226
RALLYE MONTE-CARLO
226
5C-62968

redesigned the block for their 3.8 in 1957). He also cut his chassis in half and grafted on the entire rear end of a C type Jaguar (the 1951 Le Mans-winning competition version) and extensively lightened the machine. With an airscoop in place of the right-hand headlight, it was the first of the modsports XKs. Jaguar's then public relations officer Bob Berry took over from Howorth as the top man in club racing in the mid-nineteen-fifties with MWK 120, one of the four Superleggera-style ultra-lightweight XKs built as standbys for Le Mans in 1951. Then came jet bomber pilot Dick Protheroe in the "Old Egyptian", an XK unearthed near the Pyramids which survived numerous horrific crashes to win countless events to the smell of burning brake linings and the shudder of buckling brake drums.

Abroad, one of the first XKs to reach Australia covered 6000 miles in its first week, including averaging 91.3 mph for the 965 miles from Darwin to Alice Springs in the hands of owner Les Taylor and observer Dick Rendle. It was an unofficial record for which Taylor was fined £18 with £2 costs for dangerous driving, speeding, driving without a Northern Territory licence and for driving a car not registered in the Northern Territory! Nevertheless, like all record attempts, it provided priceless publicity for Jaguars.

All this must have seemed like a joyride compared to Whitehead's experiences in Australia's first twenty-four-hour race at Mount Druitt in 1954. Incessant rain covered parts of the old airstrip in thick mud, the worst quagmire being in the pits, an area of grass with naked light bulbs strung across it. The entry ranged from Whitehead's C type and an XK120 Fixed-head coupé driven by the "mature" Mrs Doris Anderson to a Humber Hawk and a Fiat Topolino. The C type, co-driven by Tony Gaze and Alf Barrett, howled away from the opposition, horn blaring and lights flashing as it lapped baulking backmarkers. Mrs Anderson's XK, co-driven by Bill Pitt, constantly over-revved. Ray Lewis's Mark V Jaguar saloon spent much time in the mud of the pits having repeated bearing changes. Eventually it was forced to complete twenty of the twenty-four hours running on only five cylinders, the offending piston and con-rod having been removed. Meanwhile the C type thundered on through potholes and mud, averaging fifty-seven mph. Then the hard-driven XK's engine moved so far forward in the chassis that it cracked its carburetters against the steering column. An appeal over the public address system brought forward a spectator whose car was stripped for spares. Then, after eight hours, with the C type miles ahead, it suffered repeated suspension failures. Meanwhile, the coupé, still revving furiously, with wheels spinning, moved into the lead, as Dick Shaw's Holden bent an axle in a pothole.

left
As late as 1953, the XK120 was still one of the fastest cars in the classic 1000-mile Mille Miglia road race round Italy, as the number of this roadster driven by its Swiss entrant Gianati indicates. The smallest cars started from Brescia at 9 pm with the rest of the 488 starters following at one-minute intervals with their numbers indicating the starting time right through the night to 6.30 am. Only 283 cars survived this race of attrition with Gianati's Jaguar well behind the winner, Marzotto in a works Ferrari that cost ten times as much

below left
Jaguar XKs showed their versatility by competing even in the Monte Carlo Rally in tortuous conditions more suited to saloon cars. Here the Americans Nuthall and Albrecht set off from Munich in their German-registered XK140 Fixed-head coupé complete with Wyresole all-weather tyres on the roof for when the going got really tough. Despite being handicapped by a swinging door they took sixth place on the La Turbie hillclimb near Monte Carlo before being eliminated. Soon after, Ulsterman Ronnie Adams won the rally in a Mark VII saloon

17
LOE 3

The XKs were still popular cars even in international rallies as late as 1956. Here a 120 Fixed-head driven by Grounds and Johnson outcorners one of its rivals, a Triumph TR3, at Zandvoort in the Tulip Rally. Both these rapid cars were handicapped out of the Dutch event, however, with Grounds finishing seventy-fifth behind the winning Austin A30 of father-and-son team Raymond and E. W. H. Brookes

Amid all the excitement of the battle royal between Jaguar and Aston Martin factory cars at Le Mans in 1956, a rather ordinary looking XK140 Fixed-head coupé, pictured here at Arnage, lapped consistently and without drama. Its amateur crew of R. Walshaw and P. Bolton were helped out with a bit of advice from Ecurie Ecosse patron David Murray—but he was too busy with the winning D type to stop them refuelling one lap too soon after twenty-one hours; their gallant attempt ended in disqualification while in fourteenth place, an extraordinary achievement

As the chequered flag fell with Mrs Anderson victorious, several other cars lurched over the line, including the C type, which won the over 3000 cc open car class. Those were the days of real Group One cars . . . and those were the days in 1956 that a standard XK140 Fixed-head coupé with 25,000 miles on the clock and little more than a good service, was only eliminated at Le Mans while holding fourteenth place after twenty-one hours when its amateur team refuelled too early.

XKs continued to give a good account of themselves in minor club events, in the hands of drivers such as Rob Beck, Eric Brown (who lent his car to Jackie Stewart on at least one occasion), Dave Cottingham and John Harper, particularly as the disc brakes from XK150S and Mark IX saloons and D type racing engines were being fitted to the early, lightweight, XK120s. The XK140 saw comparatively little competition use, other than in the hands of Appleyard towards the end of his rallying career in the mid-nineteen-fifties. Later, in 1960, David Hobbs began a long driving career in an incredible XK140 Drop-head coupé registered TAC 743, with disc brakes all round, XK150S engine and automatic gearbox. It invariably cornered "very extravagantly" according to *Motor Sport*, "with bags of smoke and wheelspin". Clearly Hobbs was out to prove the durability of his Hobbs-Mechamatic transmission, winning all manner of club events! Later, in the mid-nineteen-sixties, this extraordinary car was rebodied as a fixed-head coupé to be campaigned in hillclimbs, and as late as 1965 an XK140 Roadster driven by Ron McConkey won a Sports Car Club of America national championship. A variety of XK140s proved reasonably competitive in international rallies during the late nineteen-fifties despite weighing much more than many of their competitors and more than the earlier 120s. The same factors worked against the XK150 in competition, despite its four-wheel disc brakes—lighter XK120s fitted with 150 discs and sometimes the rack-and-pinion steering from a 140 or 150 proved to be much quicker. Jack Lambert, former 500 cc king Don Parker and Warren Pearce with a modified, alloy-bodied example enjoyed the most success with the 150 during the late nineteen-fifties and early sixties.

Then, just as we thought we had seen the last of the XKs as top crowd-pullers, a real Jekyll and Hyde hit the British tracks! It started quite innocuously as a 1954 drop-head—the most sedate of XK120s—with a 3.8-litre Mark X saloon engine and wide alloy wheels which were in vogue at the time. It was a typical clubman's car, but it won numerous races in 1969 in the hands of its owner, John Pearson, and John Harper: then it changed its character completely in 1970. It was stripped to the chassis, moulds were taken from the original body panels, and a complete glass-fibre body made. A new floor and transmission tunnel were fabricated from aluminium and the whole lot mounted on the original, barely changed, chassis. A replica glass-fibre hood completed the effects. When finished, the car looked almost exactly as it had the year before except that, when viewed against a strong light, it glowed!

Throughout the nineteen-fifties, club events were terrorized by a battered XK120 Roadster called the Ancient Egyptian, driven by jet bomber pilot Dick Protheroe. Many were the races it won and many were the races it lost, to the detriment of brake drums, linings, course markers, hay bales and scenery

At this stage little was done to the suspension, except to give the front wheels half a degree of negative camber and to locate the back axle with radius arms. The engine was brought up to E type modified sports car specification with a big valve head and triple Weber 45DCOE carburetters on a Tecalemit-Jackson fuel-injection manifold.

The season started with a crash and continued with a series of engine failures until "Plastic" Pearson got his fearsome beast into the swing of things—and promptly started mopping up modsports lap records. There was nothing, not even an E type, that could hold it on the straights, and through the bends Pearson had only to lean on Lotus Elans to scatter them in his wake. All through 1971 and 1972 the car's specification was improved, eventually winding up with Lola T142 coil spring damper units front and rear in place of the hefty old torsion bars and leaf springs, and the radiator in the boot for better traction.

The effect on crowds throughout Britain was electric—here was an antique projectile making the modern racers look silly! Pearson even experimented with supercharging before moving over to a Lotus Elan—but with changes in the regulations and the demise of the plastic XK much of the interest in modsports events evaporated.

Thoroughbred racing with wheel widths limited to six inches and fairly standard bodywork was taking over; much to the delight of the owners of run-of-the-mill XKs.

Their register within the Jaguar Drivers' Club—a sort of club within a club—had started this style of racing in the early nineteen-seventies when they found that their XKs had run out of events. Their championships were designed for production cars built between 1946 and 1959—which

Peter Butt in his XK120 Roadster gallantly tries to hold Peter Farquharson's 5½-litre Chrysler-engined Allard special at the Brighton Speed Trials. Farquharson crossed the line first in 26.23 seconds—but Jaguar had their revenge; J. A. Playford beat him in the big sports car class with 26.03 seconds in a Le Mans lightweight E type. The year? 1962 . . . and the XK120 was still good for a burn-up

meant a re-creation of the sports car racing of the 1950s with Triumph TRs, MGAs, Big Healeys, Aston Martins and Jaguar XKs to the fore. The races were divided into three classes, up to 1650 cc, 1651 cc to 2700 cc, and 2701 cc and over. The XK120 proved to be the perfect car for the top class and for winning overall—with the chief opposition coming from a Big Healey driven by the vastly experienced John Chatham, an Aston Martin DB4 driven by former rallycross king Dave Preece and the Triumph TR3 of Reg Woodcock; other opposition for the XK120s was provided by the incredibly rapid XK150 Fixed-head coupé of housewife Sylvia Rouse. Then Preece passed his Aston over to Mrs Rouse and took the wheel of a remarkable, and battered, 120 Roadster prepared and entered by Oldham and Crowther that had already had a spectacular history, first in the hands of one proprietor, Ruth Oldham, and then the other, Martin Crowther. Gradually the battle for outright wins developed into a duel between Harper and Preece, Harper first in his Forward Engineering-prepared left-hand-drive alloy-bodied 120 Roadster registered PCY 189L, and then in Tester Engineering's right-hand-drive roadster, OLT 393. Oldham and Crowther spent much time repairing and respraying Preece's car, WPU 207, and even more time developing the rear suspension and increasing the engine's power until their car emerged on top in 1978 after years of XK dominance by Harper.

Initially these thoroughbred racers were fitted with extra leaves in their rear springs and radius arms to combat axle tramp; unfortunately these springs tended to make the cars somewhat tail happy, much to the delight of the spectators. Now the trend is towards softening the rear end with extra

The ex-David Hobbs automatic XK140, rebodied to look rather like an E type, leads Sylvia Rouse in her XK150 and John "Metal" Pearson in his ex-Lofty England XK120 Fixed-head coupé at the Jaguar Drivers' Club spring Silverstone meeting in 1972

John Harper in his XK120 Fixed-head racer takes Tom Leake's exotic Aston Martin DB4GT Zagato in the "Clubman's Le Mans", the 750 Motor Club's Six-hour Relay Race sponsored by *Cars and Car Conversions* magazine at Silverstone in 1970. Despite the valiant attempts of Harper and company, the Aston team snatched victory on handicap in the closing minutes

25B
GKY
907

Simple modsports car for which the formula was designed: James Mehew's Jaguar XK140 Fixed-head coupé sporting a towbar, pictured at Silverstone in 1971, . . . and the king of them all, John "Plastic" Pearson's ultra-sophisticated glass-fibre bodied coil-sprung projectile which took lap records all over Britain until new regulations outlawed it in 1973. In the three years from 1970 this XK120 Drop-head coupé did more to enthrall crowds than almost any other racing car in Britain. It is sadly missed

Thoroughbred racing in the mid-nineteen-seventies: Former Rallycross king Dave Preece cornering hard in the formidable Oldham and Crowther XK120 Roadster, with Dave Cottingham's 120 Fixed-head and two Aston Martins, a DB4 and Zagato, hard on his heels. Eventually there was little that could stay with Preece other than Harper in a variety of XK120 Roadsters, or John Chatham in his Big Healey on a wet track

location by Watts linkage and more damping from Armstrong Formula One telescopics rather than the old lever arm shock absorbers. A variety of anti-roll bars was used and at least as much science devoted to setting up the car as in any other branch of racing. Front suspensions remain basically standard, except that the torsion bars are wound down as far as possible, wheels are given up to $1\frac{1}{4}$ degrees of negative camber, and bronze bushes are used in place of Metalastik rubber bushes for better feel. The rack-and-pinion steering gear from an XK150 further improves these 120 Roadsters. Bodywork is in aluminium as with most other historic racers, and Borrani wheels help to cool the disc brakes fitted all round. The engines are 3.8s giving at least 300 bhp with carbs as big as 58 mm Webers or Dellortos and six-branch exhaust manifolds at more than 7000 rpm—a far cry from the 160 bhp produced at 5750 rpm by the first twin SU XK120s in 1949! Getting enough fuel to the front of today's racers can be critical, so petrol lines and pumps are frequently modified. Overheating has been a major problem, combated on the 120s prepared by Tester, Forward Engineering and Oldham and Crowther by the use of series one E type header tanks mounted behind the engine with the flow through the water rail reversed.

Despite all these modifications, the cars can be used on the road! Harper has been seen to drive a hundred miles home with only the addition of a silencer and trade plates. There will never be another like the XK; a car that has dominated one class or another of competition for thirty years, and is still so docile that you can potter home through the lanes. . . .

Definitive picture of one of the most beautiful Jaguars and greatest sports car driver: Stirling Moss drives his C type to victory in the Tourist Trophy at Dundrod, Northern Ireland. It was like a lap of honour before the home crowds after the great victory at Le Mans. As ever, Moss's car bears his lucky number seven. Walker's C type finished second

Chapter 4
C and D grand slam

Mungo Heynes and Bill Lyons hardly slept that night in June 1950. They were watching their pet XK lapping like clockwork at Le Mans. Now that can be a boring business on those lengthy laps. You only saw your car for a few seconds every five minutes or so. That's less than a couple of minutes every hour; less than an hour during the twenty-one the car lasted. But Heynes and Lyons weren't wasting their time. They had been planning things at night since their fire-watching days. They spent most of their twenty "free" hours at Le Mans that year thinking of the future. And when the XK's run was over, Lyons said: "You know, Heynes, I think we could win this event with a real racing car."

"I think we could, sir," said Heynes. There were delays, but in a frantic six months before Le Mans 1951, Heynes built the first Jaguar designed purely for racing. It was amazing what he achieved in such a short time, having spent the previous six months developing the Mark VII saloon! Engine power was increased by twenty-five per cent, to 210 bhp, with a new high-compression head, bigger carburetters and better exhaust; the crankcase was also reinforced. But these modifications—enough to occupy most development teams for considerably more than six months—paled into insignificance against Heynes's other achievements. He chalked out a new chassis on the development shop floor, designed a new torsion bar rear suspension and clothed the whole in a new body. What's more, he made it all work! The new Jaguars, bearing the chassis numbers XKC (for competition), had been built with one thing in mind; to win at Le Mans. Before that fateful twenty-four hours in June 1951, people other than rabid motoring enthusiasts were still associating the name Jaguar with an obscure breed of South American jungle cat. The times were a-changing. . . .

Moss demonstrated his athleticism from the very start, sprinting across the track at Le Mans to engage in a headlong duel with the Buenos Aires taxi driver Froilan

"For those in peril on the C . . ." Reserve Tony Rolt hangs out the tail of his C type on the way to a lap record in the 1951 Tourist Trophy race after taking over the number one car from Leslie Johnson when he fell ill. Rolt fought his way up to the fourth place and completed the winning team—the start of a great career in Jaguars

Gonzalez in what amounted to a $4\frac{1}{2}$-litre grand prix Talbot with cycle wings. Within five laps Moss had disposed of the Pampas Bull and the much-vaunted Ferraris were trailing. After four hours, Jaguar domination appeared to be complete, with Moss securely in the lead, Biondetti second and Walker third.

But no great story is complete without drama and this race had it all; after four hours the oil pressure needle on Biondetti's C type sank before Johnson even had a chance to drive. Bad vibrations had broken an oil pipe and its race was run; obviously the same thing could happen to the other two untried cars. With bated breath, Britons everywhere waited for the BBC radio to report the worst. And they did: by midnight the leading C type of Moss and Jack Fairman had stopped in a pool of oil . . . how long could the farmers Walker and Whitehead keep going in the lonely new leader? Twenty-four hours without missing a beat, that was the answer! Their Jaguar won by seventy-seven miles from the only surviving Talbot of Meyrat and Mairesse with Macklin and Thompson third in an Aston Martin. Cat lovers never recovered; from that day the name Jaguar meant a car that set standards of its own for speed, beauty and aggression. The other cat was relegated to its natural habitat and Jaguar car sales soared by thirty per cent.

The rest of the season was like a lap of honour, with Moss winning the Tourist Trophy again, with Walker second in another C type, and reserve Rolt fourth to complete the winning team. Moss also set the lap record for the difficult

Sixteen laps and Scotsman Ian Stewart becomes the first to retire of the three ill-fated 1952 Le Mans C type drivers. Here he surveys his stricken car as the Jowett Jupiter of Becquart and Wilkins purrs on to become the only finisher in the 1500 cc class

Dundrod circuit and confirmed his place in the following year's works team. Minor victories followed with the next major sports car race, the Silverstone production event, falling to the inevitable Moss. By then, Jaguars were deeply involved in testing the revolutionary new disc brakes with Norman Dewis, a vastly underrated driver who had taken over from Sutton as chief tester. Dewis, who thought little of driving five or six hundred miles a day, seven days a week, testing variations on the new brakes, later told *XK Bulletin* editor Phil Porter:

"We were ready to go to the Mille Miglia in 'fifty-two with a brake which we knew very little about, but we thought it was the right sort of race, with the distance to be covered, so that we could see, first, just how the brake did perform, and, second, what the pad life would be."

Porter questioned that it must have been a little bit worrying wondering whether the brakes were going to work as the car descended some mountain or other . . . . "Yes, that's right," said Dewis. "Stirling Moss, for whom I co-drove, was briefed on the situation that we hadn't raced it before, although he knew all the work we'd done, and, of course, he was very interested in it, because to have something that your competitors haven't got is worth quite a lot in a race. Fortunately, we didn't strike any great problems with the brake. It was certainly a very great feature when we were racing against Caracciola in the Merc. We caught up with him and, I don't know how long we were with him, it was difficult to say, but probably about sixty or seventy miles; we were able to outbrake him every

SODA
78

Manzon and Moss in the C type and Gordini (number fifty-six) were duelling for the lead in the 1952 Monaco Grand Prix when they crashed at St Devote after Mascarenhas's Allard had spilled fuel over the track. They virtually buried Parnell's Aston Martin, which had stopped among the straw bales before Hume's Allard (number eighty-four) joined the melée. Only the Jaguar could restart after a spectator helped move it clear—but the British driver was disqualified twenty-two laps later as he chased the winner, Marzotto in a Ferrari, for receiving assistance; and the crowds howled for justice for the gallant British combination

Hamilton hurls his C type past the pits at Le Mans on his way to the epic win of 1953, with Moss and Walker second in another C type; Whitehead and Ian Stewart fourth and Laurent and de Tornaco ninth in other C types. Jaguars had started four cars and finished four cars. It was the year of the C type

time. He couldn't understand it at all, we could see him look every time, he was 'decelling' like mad, and under his braking we went by still flat, and then put the brakes on in front of him. He said afterwards it was incredible, several times he didn't think the car was going to stop."

Obviously those sixty or so miles had a profound effect on Caracciola; he went back to Mercedes with tales about wonderful Jaguar brakes. Moss, in turn, went back to Jaguars with tales about the fantastic speed of the Mercedes, which cancelled out the advantage of his new brakes. And Jaguars panicked. If what Moss said was right—and he had seen it at first hand—the Mercedes was going to walk away from the Jaguar on the long straight at Le Mans. Frantically, Jaguars fitted beautifully streamlined new bodies in a desperate attempt to improve their top speed; this entailed revision of the cooling system. And equally hastily, Mercedes rigged up an air brake on one of their cars; the difference was that the Mercedes modifications worked and Jaguar's cooling system did not. The three 1952 C types were all in the dead car park within three and a half hours and that was the last anybody saw of that bodywork or cooling system. Needless to say, Mercedes won—and Jaguars were even more determined than ever to avenge the indignity; it was like fighting the war all over again.

The year 1952 was a significant one for a variety of reasons so far as the motor racing fan was concerned: it was the year Mr Average defiled his car with awful clip-on bug deflectors; it was the year that Jaguars failed at Le Mans; and it was the year that competition was so poor in Formula One that they ran the Monaco Grand Prix for sports cars. Ferrari fielded their usual strong team, Aston Martin had their new DB3, a lone works Gordini looked promising; Moss and Wisdom were there with standard-bodied C types. Most of them collided at one particular corner, leading to Moss's disqualification, but Wisdom gave Jaguars their only place in a major grand prix: sixth. Moss was back in the winning slot at Rheims, however, and the Jersey road race, like Monaco, switched from open-wheeled racing cars, fell to Ian Stewart in one of the first production C types, entered by the Ecurie Ecosse.

Soon after a new form of racing came to Britain: the Goodwood Nine-Hour based on the Le Mans epic. This type of endurance racing had never been seen in Britain before and the prospect of watching cars race at night was the prime attraction. In fact, it formed the grand finale with the chequered flag falling at midnight! It really was a mini-Le Mans, with Ferrari and Talbot well represented beside

Careful planning and teamwork executed with military precision is essential at Le Mans. Here one mechanic refuels the Rolt/Hamilton C type in 1953 as another removes a rear wheel, a third checks oil and water, and a fourth in the background carries a fresh wheel to the man doing the changing. Watching it all is a French scrutineer, wearing his traditional beret. Many people considered the cameramen something of a nuisance. We should be grateful that they were there

works C types and Aston Martin DB3s. Rolt and Hamilton's C type led for the first eight laps on a rain-soaked course until Parnell, exploiting the Aston's superior handling, took the lead, followed by Abecassis in another Aston, Moss's C type, Baird's Ferrari and Whitehead's C type. As the road dried, the Jaguars powered to the front in 1-2-3 formation; then the first blow fell. Whitehead crashed, letting Parnell into third place, with Salvadori taking over Baird's Ferrari in fourth place, Abecassis fifth and another Aston, driven by Pat Griffith and Peter Collins, sixth. Soon after, at the three-hour mark, Parnell's DB3 burst into flames on refuelling, injuring three of the pit staff and giving the packed grandstands even more to talk about. As the leading C types stopped for fuel and tyres, Tom Cole and Graham Whitehead in another Ferrari moved up to third place, but as night fell Collins and Griffith had fought back to third in the Aston.

Suddenly the Rolt/Hamilton C type shed a wheel and Salvadori took second place in his Ferrari; the Moss/Walker C type broke its suspension and Salvadori was in the lead! As the Jaguar mechanics worked like slaves to repair a fractured A-bracket, the Ferrari failed to restart after a pit stop. Collins took the lead and held it to the end with a sick-sounding Aston. Cole took second place and

Kaplan and Boss kept their C type looking immaculate on its way to ninth overall and second in class in the 1954 Sebring Twelve Hour race, won by Moss and Bill Lloyd in an OSCA; but fellow C type exponents Benett and McKenna fell foul of a sandbank and finished twentieth looking decidedly secondhand

Salvadori restarted for third; Gerard and Clarke were fourth in a Frazer-Nash and Moss made it back to fifth after losing thirty-six minutes. Jaguars had been beaten before their home crowds, but their popularity had never been higher—you could actually buy a C type then and many were on their way to America.

Early campaigners in the States in 1953 included Phil Hill and Sherwood Johnston, whose chief opposition came from cycle-winged Allards powered by a variety of large American V8s, chiefly Cadillac or Lincoln. But these Allard J2s were fast becoming relics of a bygone age with little extra performance to be squeezed from them; soon even their fastest exponents, such as Bill Pollak, were into C type Jaguars. Other successful C type drivers in America included Sterling Edwards and a youngster from Kansas called Masten Gregory, who had had a brief flirtation with an Allard. Soon he, too, was into a C type, hammering it from track to track across the country. One of the most spectacular events of many that were to follow in Gregory's career happened at Brooklyn's Floyd Bennett Field in late autumn. It was a real Indian summer with temperatures as high as 120 degrees Fahrenheit recorded at the old airbase. And just when the sun was at its zenith, Gregory spun his white C type, splitting the fuel tank and scrambling out just

Duncan Hamilton was lucky to escape with his life when his C type hit a lamp post in the third Portuguese Grand Prix in 1953 before slewing across the road into the position shown in the picture. The crash, caused by an errant amateur in a 4.1-litre Ferrari, cut off much of Oporto's power supply. Hamilton says that when he left the road at 125 mph he deliberately rammed the pylon head-on rather than allow the car to hit it side on, "to keep the mass of metal between me and the accident". Wise advice gleaned from Alberto Ascari . . .

All day, all night, Rolt and Hamilton hammered on in their D type on its debut at Le Mans in 1954. As the heavens opened at dawn, in this picture, they began to catch the monstrous Ferrari driven by Gonzalez, but he drew away again when the track dried to establish a 105-second lead at the end

LUCAS
LUCAS
MARCHAL
VEEDOL
14

OKV 3 in one of its many roles: as a 2.4-litre handicap special with stoneblasted nose in the 1954 Dundrod TT. Moss and Whitehead tried hard, but were handicapped by engine trouble and by hitting a bank (the grass kind, there were both on that circuit). Eventually Moss pushed OKV 3 over the line for eighteenth place. D types were never a success with engines of less than 3.4 litres

in time to watch it go up in smoke. However, he was not short of a dollar or two, and somehow managed to persuade another competitor, one H. W. Wessells III, to sell him his brand new red C type. At the drop of the flag, Gregory outsprinted the others in the Le Mans start and howled into the lead; sadly, his rear suspension gave out—the old A-bracket trouble—and Bill Spear's brutal 4.1-litre Ferrari won. But a new road racing star was on his way. . . .

By 1953, Jaguars had perfected their disc brakes, too, and solved minor lubrication problems which had eliminated them from races such as the Mille Miglia. They were able to face one of the most formidable fields ever assembled at Le Mans with some confidence. Strangely, the C types were fancied by few; they had been beaten by Ferrari and Aston Martin in the International Trophy at Silverstone just before the event and the new Ferraris were certainly impressive. But once more the C types showed that Le Mans belonged to them; within four laps Moss had outbraked Gigi Villoresi's massive 4.5-litre Ferrari for the lead. After that it was a battle between the Ferrari's immense

acceleration and the Jaguar's fantastic braking, with their top speeds about equal. But it looked like 1951 all over again when Moss pulled in with fuel feed problems. However, Rolt and Hamilton rose to the occasion.

They had spent the previous night drowning their sorrows when they thought they had been disqualified for an accidental breach of practice regulations; then they found that Lyons had somehow persuaded the French authorities to let them race. Gallons of black coffee laced with pick-me-ups got them to the line; and carried them to victory twenty-four hours later, with the Ferrari falling by the wayside with a burned-out clutch, Moss having his fuel lines cleared to fight back into second place, and Briggs Cunningham driving his all-American giant into third place. To emphasize Jaguar's superiority, the C type averaged 105 mph—the first time that Le Mans had been won at more than one hundred miles an hour.

Victories and honourable defeats followed thick and fast as C types fought it out with the best the world could offer; Moss and Whitehead won the Rheims Twelve Hour, and

Briggs Cunningham in the white shirt checks last-minute details on his D type with one of its drivers, Phil Walters, before the bonnet straps are tightened after scrutineering for the 1955 Le Mans race. The Cunningham/Walters combination was one of the most successful in America during the golden years of road racing

Opposite lock all the way as Hawthorn fights his slipping, sliding D type along the rough roads of Dundrod in the 1955 Tourist Trophy race. He set fastest lap at 94.67 mph for the 7.43 mile circuit, but ended up crossing the finishing line on foot when his engine blew after eighty-two laps of the eighty-four-lap race, most of them spent in the lead with Desmond Titterington

second place went to the Ecurie Ecosse C types of Scott-Douglas and Guy Gale in the Spa Twenty-Four Hour race, and Ian Stewart and Salvadori in the 1000 kilometres at the Nurburgring. Stewart won numerous club races and finished third with Whitehead in the Goodwood Nine Hour, the factory cars having been eliminated with lubrication problems while leading.

By 1954, the Ecurie Ecosse were developing into an unofficial Jaguar works team, winning twelve top-flight international races, with eighteen places from seventeen events as far apart as Barcelona and Buenos Aires; other highly successful private entrants included Hamilton in OVC 915 when he wasn't driving a works car, and Head in the ex-Wisdom C type, MDU 212. They were the real privateers, covering the Continent from Spain to Scandinavia with cars full of spares, wives, dinner suits and crash helmets. The C type was the last of the racing sports cars that you could drive straight from Dundrod to the Dorchester, then on to the Nurburgring and the Hotel Negresco, in Nice.

The D type was the first Jaguar designed solely for racing. It was so beautiful that it rendered everything else obsolete when it appeared at Le Mans in 1954. It was built like an aeroplane with a body and chassis just like a fuselage without wings. Why, it even had a fin! The running gear was substantially the same as that of the C type, and well tested at that; there were all manner of detail improvements, such as dry sump lubrication to eliminate the oil surge that had run bearings in races like the Goodwood Nine Hour.

In many ways, the D type's debut bore a remarkable resemblance to the previous races run by Jaguars at Le Mans. Again it was brute force (a 4.9-litre Formula One-based Ferrari equally at home on cinders or cement) versus science (in the form of the 3.4-litre D type, designed specifically for the long straights of Le Mans). Neither had the advantage. Even their fastest practice times were the same.

In the race itself, Moss was once more Jaguar's pacemaker, although he merely stayed with the Ferraris at first. Then clogged fuel filters delayed the Coventry team before brake trouble and mechanical ailments eliminated Moss and Wharton. However, Rolt and Hamilton in the third car were still full of fight, ploughing on relentlessly till there was only one Ferrari left, that of Gonzalez and Trintignant. The Argentinian star drove his fearsome open machine like Ben Hur in a chariot race, but man and machine were weakening. Gonzalez had neither eaten nor slept for two days and the thundering V12, capable of churning out 100 bhp more than Jaguar's straight six when at its best, was down on compression. It took longer to restart with every pit stop and the Jaguar crept closer until it was delayed by an accident with a baulking backmarker. Still the relentless pursuit went on until the Pampas Bull called on his last reserves of strength and won by 105 seconds, with Jaguar sharing the glory in second place.

It was as good as winning the race, which Wharton and Whitehead did in any case the following weekend in the Rheims Twelve Hour. Again, Rolt and Hamilton were second, this time after having been rammed by Behra's Gordini. The next big race was the Tourist Trophy, which

right
Hawthorn leads Fangio in the early stages of the 1955 Le Mans race before disaster struck. The picture shows clearly the revised long nose of the 1955 works D type with curved windshield moulded neatly into the headrest and tailfin. Hawthorn's windshield was slightly lower than others; he preferred it that way for increased visibility

below
Just like an aeroplane about to take off . . . Hawthorn hits more than 170 mph in his D type on the way to victory at Le Mans in 1955. He was six feet tall and his helmet projected into the slipstream; smaller drivers were immersed in the D type's interior

left
Mike Hawthorn, with familiar bow tie under his racing jacket and the strain of tragedy and twenty-four hours etched on his face, accepts congratulations on winning the 1955 Le Mans race. Ivor Bueb, on the right, hangs on to the victory bouquet before they drive off from the finishing line in their D type

Above
Swaters corners the Ecurie Belge D type at Le Mans in 1956. The Belgians were among Jaguar's greatest and most consistent supporters, Laurent and de Tornaco finishing ninth in 1953; Laurent and Swaters fourth in 1954; Claes and Swaters third in 1955; Swaters and Rousselle fourth in 1956 and Frère and Rousselle fourth in 1957

right
Ron Flockhart takes the Ecurie Ecosse D type to victory at Le Mans in 1956; it was a race of faulty fuel injection for Hawthorn's D type, full-width windscreens for everybody, and a limit on tank capacity that meant cars had to be capable of at least twelve mpg. Strangely, it was the second-placed Aston Martin of Moss and Collins that was closest to the border line in this respect

left
Mechanics work feverishly on the fuel injection system of Hawthorn and Bueb's D type in the pits at Le Mans in 1956; it took them an hour to cure the trouble, but Hawthorn and Bueb fought back to sixth position at the end, taking the lap record at 115.812 mph in the process

The Ecurie Ecosse started a really ambitious international racing programme in 1957, entering two D types in the Buenos Aires 1000 kilometre sports car race for Ninian Sanderson and Roberto Mieres, and Ron Flockhart with an un-named Argentinian driver; the mystery man never got a drive because Flockhart hit a lamp post in practice. Then Sanderson was hit in the face by a bird at high speed in the surviving D type, but Mieres, pictured here, took over and drove "with spirit" to take fourth place. Gregory, Castellotti and Musso won in a Ferrari

exposed the D type's great weakness. It never ran well on an engine smaller than 3.4 litres, and could manage only fifth place with a 2.4-litre unit intended to beat the handicapper. Jaguar's next star was Mike Hawthorn, signed when Moss was lured away to Mercedes in 1955. Hawthorn was as English as they come, frequently racing in a tweed jacket and bow tie! He was also one of the fastest drivers the world has seen, promptly winning for Jaguar at Sebring with Phil Walters, in 1955.

This event marked the first involvement of the great American sportsman Briggs Cunningham with Jaguars—a partnership that was to continue throughout the glory years. It was really the taxman that got the millionaire yachtsman involved; apparently there was trouble in offsetting the huge sums he had poured into his other hobby, Cunningham cars, so Cunningham and Lyons did a deal. Jaguar wanted to promote their cars in the proper manner in the States and Cunningham had to engage in some sort of business activity to satisfy the Government. The taxman's attitude simply would not bear the very substantial losses involved in making and racing the Cunningham cars when it was obvious that they would never be sold in quantity. So Briggs became a car salesman, wholeheartedly promoting and racing works Jaguars. Lyons was happy; there was nobody better at promoting his image in America, and nobody better at preparing his car for American conditions than Cunningham's renowned engineer, Alfred Momo. Cunningham could even supply a top American road racer, Phil Walters. . . .

above
Sanderson drives the Ecurie Ecosse's spare D type, a short-nosed car, in the Nurburgring 1000 kilometres in May 1957; the plan was to use two or three long-nosed cars for most races, with the third long-nosed, or the short-nosed car, for spares while the others were being maintained or repaired. Obviously the Ecurie Ecosse were saving one of their best cars for Le Mans the following month. Sanderson and Jock Lawrence finished sixteenth in the German event, with team-mates Flockhart and Jack Fairman eighth and Bueb and Lawrence eleventh behind the winning Aston Martin. The prize and starting money from this event financed the highly successful trip to Le Mans . . .

left
Bueb and Sanderson's Ecurie Ecosse Jaguar fights its way round the Nurburgring in 1958; D types were never successful on this circuit, their suspension being unable to cope with the demands of a tortuous surface, having been designed for the billiard table at Le Mans. What happened to Bueb and Sanderson? They retired with severe suspension maladies . . .

Le Mans was the next great race for the Jaguar works team, with a thrilling duel between Hawthorn and Juan-Manuel Fangio in a Mercedes-Benz. They raced neck and neck till disaster struck as Fangio's team-mate, Pierre Levegh, collided with Macklin's Austin-Healey and careered into the crowd, killing eighty-two people. Moss took over the leading Mercedes and Bueb jumped into the Jaguar in place of the shocked Hawthorn, who had been involved in the incident leading up to the accident. Gradually their rivals, Maglioli, Castellotti and Trintignant in Ferraris, Brooks and Salvadori in Aston Martins, and the Jaguars of Walters and Beaumont, quit that tragic track. Then Mercedes withdrew, leaving the D type laps ahead, a lead it held to the end, with only Valzano's Maserati, Collins and Frère in an Aston Martin, and the Belgian D type of Swaters and Claes anywhere near. Jaguars had been covered in glory the year before.

David Murray (under the A of Jaguar) supervises operations as the 1957 Le Mans-winning 3.8-litre D type stops for fuel and a change of drivers. Flockhart can be seen waiting to take the driving seat vacated by Bueb as tuning ace Wilkie Wilkinson refuels the car

This year the glory was clouded by disaster.

The tragedy had far-reaching effects on motor racing. Many races were cancelled on safety grounds, including two world championship events, so the next round, the Tourist Trophy, assumed even greater importance. All the top sports cars were there, including one D type for Hawthorn and Ulsterman Desmond Titterington. Disaster struck again—three drivers were killed in crashes on the notoriously difficult Dundrod circuit. But the D type fought for the lead all the way until the last lap, when it seized, giving Mercedes a 1-2-3 victory. In lesser races, Ecurie Ecosse were more successful, with Titterington and Ninian Sanderson second in the Goodwood Nine Hour. Jaguar employees Bob Berry and Dewis were fifth.

In America, Johnston had progressed to a D type and celebrated with a win in the Watkins Glen Grand Prix, while C types started the rounds of club races in Britain and

"Fearless Jack" Fairman rides high on the banking at Monza in the Race of Two Worlds in 1957; an event for the best of American Indianapolis-style cars and European racers. Only Frenchman Jean Behra with a Maserati and the Ecurie Ecosse dared accept the challenge on the track—which resembled a tank testing ground in parts—because of the bumps and problems with tyres overheating on the high banking. Behra broke his back axle in practice and the D types were limited to 160 mph or their tyres blew out; some of the American cars could do 200 mph with their huge twenty-inch wheels. However, most of them fell apart on the bumps and only three could hold the Ecurie Ecosse, running in line-ahead formation of Fairman, Sanderson and Lawrence. Jimmy Bryan from Arizona won, chewing a cigar, but the Ecurie Ecosse captured the crowd's imagination and the lion's share of the £30,000 prize money

smaller events all over the world. In major events, the works D type of Hawthorn and Titterington led for the first half of the Sebring Twelve Hour in 1956, before retiring with brake trouble. This American circuit, with its long, fast straights and tight corners, had already gained a reputation for being the most punishing in the world for braking systems. Boffins were quick to note that Hawthorn's D type was equipped with the new-fangled fuel injection, a system with which Jaguars were to experiment for years. As it happened, a D type with normal induction, driven by Indianapolis winner Bob Sweikert and Jack Ensley, finished third.

In other events, the Ecurie Ecosse scored numerous wins with D types and supported the winning works D type of Hamilton and Bueb at the Rheims Twelve Hour by taking the next three places. They went one better at Le Mans when two out of the three works cars were eliminated in a first-lap crash, Sanderson and Flockhart moving up to win from the works Aston Martin of Moss and Collins. Scotsmen everywhere celebrated as only they know how.

By the end of the year, D types were scattered all over the world, with Melbourne car dealer Bib Stillwell enjoying notable success in Australia. The Ecurie Ecosse also took

over most of the works cars, easily identified by their longer-than-normal noses. One of the remaining works cars went to Cunningham to be driven into third place at Sebring behind the Maseratis of Fangio and Moss, despite more trouble with the brakes. This was a really significant car, the first of the factory 3.8 litres, having been developed by Momo. Soon this new block, as distinct from the bored-out 3.4-litre of previous years, was to be compulsory wear on competitive D types. It certainly worked well, with a fuel-injection Ecurie Ecosse car driven by Flockhart and Bueb winning Le Mans; another (3.4 carburetted) Ecurie Ecosse D type second; Lucas and Brussin third in a French 3.4 D type; Frère and Rousselle fourth in a Belgian 3.4 D type and Hamilton and Gregory sixth in Duncan's 3.8-litre D type. "It was not as though the opposition was weak, except in reliability—and it was our finest hour," said Murray, who had invested everything in the Scottish national racing team.

It was also the beginning of the end for the glorious D types, as the next year, after one gallant foray against Indianapolis cars at Monza, they ran with 3-litre engines to meet new regulations and lost all their reliability. Also the D types were being left behind by a new brand of racing

1958 was a poor vintage for Le Mans; design had stagnated with the 3-litre limit and both Ecurie Ecosse D types were out within the first hour with piston trouble; two others crashed in heavy rain, one with fatal results. However Bueb, pictured here, drove a fine race to take the lead in the night, only for Hamilton to crash their D type after nineteen hours. Gendebien and Hill won in the only Ferrari Testa Rossa to finish from the Whitehead brothers in an elderly Aston Martin, which had finished second in 1955

sports car, ultra-light specials powered by Jaguar engines that had all the power and none of the weight needed for long-distance events.

The Ecurie Ecosse soldiered on with D types at Le Mans until 1960 for mainly sentimental reasons as other ex-works cars continued to be used in all manner of events far from Britain. OKV 3, for instance, enjoyed a lot of success in the hands of John Love in South Africa, whereas others, such as XKD 558, had a far harder life. This latter D type, a 1955 model, was bought by Jim Rattenbury in Vancouver after being laid up for two years, promptly winning fifteen out of the twenty races he entered between 1957 and 1960. He then crashed the car heavily and was out of racing for four years before fitting it with Ford V8 running gear and racing it again, only to crash the long-suffering machine once more. Cars such as these then tended to disappear for a few years until the late nineteen-sixties, when historic sports car racing became all the rage. Along with better-preserved examples such as OKV 3, they were frequently rebuilt exactly as they used to be and began a new racing life.

Today, with the C types, they are among the greatest crowd-pullers from Mallory Park to Monterey, winning all manner of events just like they used to do.

Still the Ecurie Ecosse raced on at Le Mans with a D type. This example, fitted with a near-coupé top and extraordinary "luggage boot" to meet the 1960 regulations, circulated in fourth place with drivers Flockhart and Bruce Halford behind the winning Ferrari until the crankshaft broke after thirteen hours. At least it made a change from blown pistons!

above
The D type was still competitive at Le Mans in 1959, this Ecurie Ecosse example driven by Gregory and Innes Ireland holding second or third place in front of the eventual winners, Salvadori and Shelby in an Aston Martin, until it was eliminated in the fifth hour by the 3-litre engine's old bugbear, a burned piston

left
You could actually buy a D type in 1955, when this picture was taken, for a bargain price of less than £3000. How the enthusiasts would eat their hearts out to get one straight from the production line in Coventry today. These cars were, of course, the "short-nosed" production machines, and were painted in all manner of colours, even salmon pink . . .

right
Historic racing was at the height of its popularity in Britain in the early nineteen-seventies with cars such as the ex-Ecurie Ecosse D type (XKD 502) driven by Nick Faure for Hexagon of Highgate winning numerous races. This car featured independent rear suspension, using parts left over from the E2A E type prototype project, which had been fitted by Maurice Charles in the early nineteen-sixties. The car, pictured here winning the Brian Lister Trophy at Crystal Palace in 1971, set a lap record at 78.43 mph. The track has since closed, Faure has been seen more recently in a Porsche, and the car has been converted back to original specification

below
Northerners Nigel Moores of Littlewoods mail order and football pools and Anthony Bamford of JCB (excavators) gave historic racing a great impetus in 1972, organizing championship rounds at top-flight events. Here Bill Allen drives one of Moores's collection of D types in the JCB championship at Silverstone in 1972

OKV 3 revisits Le Mans in 1973 to take third place in the hands of Martin Morris; he still races this grand old car in America and Europe with considerable success. The historic event, to celebrate the fiftieth centenary of the race, was won by Willie Green's D type, and has now been perpetuated as one of the best-supported historic races in the world. Green's winning average speed of more than 100 mph would have been good enough to qualify for the twenty-four-hour race proper on the following weekend!

Phil Scragg in his element at Prescott in 1956 with his first Jaguar-engined special, the HWM-Alta, SPC 982. He recorded 50.51 seconds, to finish second in the over 3-litre class behind Ray Feilding in the original all-enveloping ex-works HWM-Jaguar (49.40 seconds). Scragg had flirted with the idea of fitting an all-enveloping body, but in the end stuck to cycle-type wings

Chapter 5
The Jaguar specials

Bill Heynes built some beautiful racing cars. The C type and the D type were just fine for long-distance events. They were big, strong and rather heavy. They had to be to last twenty-four hours, but they were a shade too heavy for short-distance circuit racing and distinctly ill at ease on any surface rougher than the billiard table at Le Mans. What's more, they were far happier in a straight line than through corners. Admittedly they had a fantastic engine and gearbox, but Heynes hadn't the time to design a lightweight specially for bumpy backwoods tracks or hillclimbs. True, there was good publicity to be gained from winning lesser events than Le Mans, but Jaguars had enough on their plate designing production cars and preparing the factory racers. So when enthusiasts started clamouring for their engines, Lyons did all he could to help. Some of these people were pretty good. They came from a generation which had grown up in another kind of competition: the Second World War. They were used to fast, lightweight devices—such as Supermarine Spitfires—and could make a fair job of a one-off car chassis. If they could build devices powered by Jaguar engines that could burn off Ferraris, Maseratis and Aston Martins, Lyons was only too happy to supply essential components and reap some of the resultant publicity. Why, he would even loan them an engine if they were sufficiently good, or sell it at a knock-down price as he did for Ecurie Ecosse.

That is why Frank Le Gallais obtained a special equipment XK engine so soon for his hillclimb car. How could he get such a splendid power unit when the average man was having to wait years for a car? Because he had been using a Jaguar Mark V pushrod engine in his hillclimb chassis and his chassis developer was not without talent. He was Alec Issigonis, who knew a thing or two about roadholding. Hadn't the great Pomeroy, an acknowledged expert on grand prix cars, said that Issigonis's brilliant new Morris Minor of 1949 had better roadholding than any of them?

right
George Abecassis's HWM-Jaguar howls past novice D. R. Bethel in his unique road-equipped Aston Martin DB3, early in 1955. Abecassis crashed heavily in the HWM soon after at Snetterton, wrecking the coachwork. It was the body intended for Scragg's HWM-Alta-Jaguar, that had first been used in 1954 with composite metal and Perspex screen and large airscoop on the bonnet, before being smoothed out as in this picture

below
The second HWM 1 was still being campaigned by owner Kirk Rylands twenty years after it was built in 1956—and, as this picture shows, was fitted with a far prettier body than the earlier car. It was similar in design to that fitted to the other works car, XPE 2

It was in 1949 that Jerseyman Le Gallais had his first real success on the Bouley Bay hillclimb with his LGS. Powered by the Mark V engine, this mid-engined, twin-girdered chassis with Citroën front suspension and rubber suspended rear swing axles, got within three seconds of the winning ERA for third place in the island's famous hillclimb. It was the start of something big for Issigonis, too. He was to use rubber in his Mini suspension ten years later. . . .

The following year, 1950, Le Gallais had his rather special XK engine and was down to ERA times, beating Walker's C type during an excursion to Prescott in 1953. Back at Bouley Bay, the LGS was unbeatable in its class, winning at Shelsley Walsh and Prescott on other occasions. Right until 1958, when it was sold for Kenyan racing and soon written off, it had all the latest equipment, including one of the fascinating "back-to-front" inlet manifolds, in which triple SU carburetters were mounted inwards so that longer induction tubes could be used.

A 2½-litre push-rod Jaguar engine similar to the 3½-litre unit used by Le Gallais in 1949 powered another particularly successful sprinter in the immediate post-war years: Gordon Parker's Jaguette. The other essential parts of this rapid machine were an MG N-type Magnette chassis with ultra-lightweight alloy body. In supercharged form, it enjoyed a number of hillclimb successes in Parker's hands before he moved on to even quicker Jaguar specials in 1952.

Scott-Brown storms to yet another win in the Crystal Palace race in 1957, in the first of the works Lister-Jaguars, based on the earlier Lister-Bristol. He won at 73.50 mph from Graham Whitehead, Les Leston, Jack Brabham and Peter Whitehead in that order, setting fastest lap at 75.82 mph

That was the year when the cult really took off. A big, raw-boned Englishman, John Heath, a couple of mechanics and a part-time welder had been building rather special racers at Heath, Walton, Motors, in conjunction with Geoffrey Taylor's Alta concern down the road from Walton, at Kingston-on-Thames. As Heath built cars, his partner, George Abecassis, endeavoured to keep the firm afloat, besides getting involved with Aston Martins. Their early projects included a trio of dual-purpose Alta-engined HWM Formula Two/sports racers in 1950. They were very fast and the engines were very fragile as Finchley motor trader Oscar Moore, Tom Meyer and Swiss rallyman Jean de Wurstemberger were to discover; but Moore liked the excellent roadholding imparted by the transverse leaf sprung chassis and dropped a hot XK engine into his car for the 1952 season. At the same time, Abecassis was doing the

same thing with a similar, obsolete Grand Prix Alta chassis for northern hillclimber Phil Scragg. The HWM-Jaguar marque had been born and Jaguar specials were heading for the big time.

Moore, in his cycle-winged projectile, registered XMC 34, proved well-nigh unbeatable in the club races of 1952. Scragg was torn between two ideals: he wanted a modern, all-enveloping racer on the lines being adopted in international competition that he could use on the road, but he still hankered after a toothpaste tube body where you could see the front wheels for better positioning on steep and twisty hillclimbs. He went as far as ordering an all-enveloping body for his Alta-Jaguar (the engine came from his smashed-up competition XK) then backed out and had HWMs fit a body like Moore's. So Heath and Abecassis were left with a surplus sports car body while they carried

Archie Scott-Brown's Lister-Jaguar was long gone when the cameraman caught Les Leston (HWM-Jaguar number 66) contesting second place with Graham Whitehead (Aston Martin DB3S number 61), his brother Peter Whitehead (Aston Martin DB3S number 62), Jack Brabham (Tojeiro-Jaguar number 65), Jim Russell (Cooper-Jaguar number 64) and Peter Mould (Jaguar C type number 60) in the unlimited sports car race at Crystal Palace in July 1957

on building single-seater HWMs for Formula Two racing. These, incidentally, had coil-sprung front suspension.

By the June of 1952 the rough-and-ready Moore had ventured where nobody on his side of the Atlantic had previously dared to tread, and had bored out his XK engine to 3.8 litres; Heath had seen enough of the Italian cars' Weber carburetters to adapt them for use with an XK engine. Already the Jaguar specials were well advanced technically.

As Moore fought it out with the works Jaguars, Abecassis was left trailing with his Aston—and by the end of the season was screwing together another HWM-Jaguar. This one had all the goodies: a single-seater chassis adapted to take Scragg's all-enveloping body—cycle wings had been outlawed for international competition by then—and fitted with a Weberized XK engine and Indianapolis-style quick-change Halibrand spur gears for the rear axle. Thus its gear ratios could be readily varied for any circuit; the registration number was, appropriately, HWM 1.

Peter Whitehead's original mark one Cooper-Jaguar was sold to Dickie Steed in 1956 after Steed wrote off his Porsche Carrera. Whitehead had little success with the Cooper, but Steed managed a number of wins in British sports car events. Here he leads Archie Scott-Brown in the Scotsman's troublesome Lister-Maserati

Mind you, they were not the only people busy with Jaguar specials in 1952. Billy Coleman had bought the Jaguette and set fastest time of the day for sports cars at the Brighton Speed Trials while that was still a top award, and he continued to compete with it until the nineteen-sixties, winning his class in 1960 and 1961. Meanwhile, Parker had bought a proprietary Buckler multi-tubular chassis meant for Ford side-valve power and fitted a supercharged XK engine! For years this car, the Jaguara, battled with everything everywhere on the club circuits and particularly for fastest time of the day with Scragg's HWM-Jaguar in the hills.

Not far from Walton-on-Thames, that hot-bed of special building, another garage proprietor, Dick Shattock, from Winkfield Row, had bought up piles of parts from the pre-war Atalanta sports car project in Staines. He built chassis to order for enthusiasts with his own torsion bar front suspension and coil-sprung rear, often selling them one half and then the other months later when they had saved up

6

enough cash. His works car, HBL 845, with aluminium cigar-shaped body and cycle wings, was reasonably fast with Lea-Francis power until he fitted it with a C type Jaguar engine in 1953, when it really took off. The car was transformed into a regular race winner when he changed the body. It is believed to have been Britain's first glass-fibre-bodied sports car, using moulds made from the rear end of an all-enveloping HWM alloy body. Shattock used the same mould for front and rear, fitting fins to the back wings of HBL 845 "so that you could tell which way it was going!" His bodies helped launch the TVR sports car concern in Blackpool and HBL went really well, especially in the wet, thanks to its novel suspension and new Michelin X radial ply tyres.

The Australians were in on the act of Jaguar special building, too, although Americans showed little interest at this point—they had plenty of home-brewed V8s and preferred to use them, even to the extent of fitting them into D types! One of the earliest Jaguar specials in Australia was Larry Humphries's Austal-Union built from the wreckage of an XK120 Roadster. It was a rough-and-ready open-wheeled machine, frequently eclipsed by another, similar, but better finished, car called the Jack Robinson Special.

More sophisticated and better streamlined cars, such as HWM 1, were taking over in 1953, with Moore abandoning his snub-nosed special. Lyons must have been delighted when Abecassis's HWM led the works Astons at one point in the Goodwood Nine Hour of 1953 and got into the first six places in the Rheims Twelve Hour. With this kind of success behind them, and the lack of a competitive British Formula One or Two engine, HWM concentrated on sports car racing for 1954.

New alloy-bodied cars were built with coil-sprung front ends and the old HWM 1 was beefed up with a steel body

above
Rare bird . . . the lovely Tojeiro-Jaguar, the second one to be registered 7 GNO and the only one to be fitted with wire wheels. Jack Brabham, Jack Fairman and Dickie Steed drove this car with some success before patron John Ogier wrote it off in October 1957

far left
Whitehead had little more success with the mark two Cooper-Jaguar, pictured here in the international sports car race at Silverstone in May 1955. Whitehead tried hard, but he trailed with an oil leak as Parnell and Salvadori walked away with the race in works Aston Martins. The mark two Cooper-Jaguar might have been better looking, but it fared no better than its predecessor

Ron Flockhart roars off into the lead in the Ecurie Ecosse Tojeiro-Jaguar (number three) to win the big Whitsun event at Goodwood in 1959. He led all the way except on laps seven, eight and nine, when a young driver called Jim Clark in the Border Reivers "knobbly" Lister (number five) took him—only to run out of petrol half-way through the twenty-one lap race. "But Clark's day will come," said *Motor Sport*. . . . Second in this picture is Bruce Halford in the "Flat Iron" Lister and fourth Graham Whitehead in a DBR1 Aston Martin with Mike Salmon about to leave the line in a D type, partly obscuring Bill de Selincourt's amazingly fast 1100 cc Lotus-Climax and Maurice Charles's D type. In the race itself, Beckaert's Lister-Jaguar finished second with Blond's Lister-Jaguar third

BP SUPER PLUS
BP ENERGOL MOTOR OIL
4
HCN 736
5
1
17
11

This famous car, the "Flat Iron" Lister, was the first Jaguar-engined car to be completed for a customer during the great production run of 1958. The customer was Dick Walsh and the registration number, HCH 736, was already well known, having been used on Austin Nurse's Lister-Bristol, giving rise to speculation that it was a rebuild of an earlier car, like Scott-Brown's MVE 303 and VPP 9. The body was unique, having been built by Maurice Gomm at Byfleet, a man responsible for many bodies on British specials over the years. The "Flat Iron" Lister was to become one of the most famous of the Cambridge cars in the hands of Halford and Clark and is still being campaigned to great effect in historic racing. It is pictured here in the hands of Gordon Lee at Crystal Palace in 1971

for long-distance racing—its old body probably going to Shattock. The Mille Miglia proved to be too hard for its suspension, but Abecassis beat the works Astons (and Jaguars) in the International Trophy Meeting at Silverstone with only Gonzalez in a Le Mans-style Ferrari ahead of him. One of the new cars, VPA 9, was quite successful in the hands of Australian Tony Gaze.

Ninth in the Silverstone race was yet another breed of "Big Cat", the Cooper-Jaguar. Peter Whitehead had been racing a Cooper-Alta in Formula Two in-between Jaguar works drives and wanted something lighter to compete with the HWMs. It was the biggest car that the Surbiton firm had been asked to build and they went to town on the reinforcements. It had a massive chassis made from numerous curved tubes, with alloy bodywork. Early attempts at running it with a shark's mouth radiator were abandoned and it was fitted with a normal nosepiece, achieving some success in Whitehead's hands. Replicas were made for northern enthusiasts Bertie Bradnack and Jack Walton. These 1954 cars had all-independent, transverse leaf-spring suspension and side exhausts rather like those on the contemporary Mercedes-Benz 300 SLRs.

New mark two versions of the Cooper-Jaguar were built for 1955 with more conventional coachwork, one being

used by Whitehead and the others going to Head and Tommy Sopwith, who had been racing an Armstrong-Siddeley-engined Allard special called the Sphynx. These cars proved to be competitive with works Jaguars on short circuits, but fractionally slower than HWM's new coil-sprung car. This had a new, more shapely body and was registered XPE 2, racing alongside the old faithful HWM 1 and VPA 9. Its drivers included Abecassis, Lance Macklin, Harry Schell and Angela Brown (daughter of Aston Martin chief David Brown), who was soon to wed Abecassis.

In the winter, Whitehead and Gaze took their Cooper and HWM cars to Australia and New Zealand, along with Leslie Marr's streamlined all-enveloping Connaught—fitted with a D type engine—to make yet another Jaguar special. It was becoming quite a local industry for the Formula Two boys, for this car was built at Send, Surrey, only a few miles from all the other Jaguar circuit specials to date.

The Cooper-Jaguar was later quite successful in the hands of Stan Jones, father of grand prix star Alan Jones. For the rest of the nineteen-fifties the HWMs and Coopers were raced with varying degrees of success in events as diverse as the Mille Miglia and club meetings. HWMs built another coil-sprung chassis for 1956, clothing it in a pretty

Stirling Moss wins the British Grand Prix meeting sports car event at Silverstone in MVE 303, just ahead of Salvadori in the 2-litre class-winning Lotus-Bristol. A duel between Moss and Gregory had been expected, but the American had been injured and his Ecurie Ecosse Tojeiro Jaguar wrecked when he leapt from the cockpit after losing his machine on a corner in practice

Ivor Bueb sets a lap record winning the unlimited sports car race at Crystal Palace in 1958 in the works "knobbly" Lister from Bruce Halford in the "Flat Iron" Lister and Graham Whitehead in his famous ex-works Aston Martin DB3S, 62 EMU. Bueb's Lister is fitted with a full-width screen to meet contemporary long-distance sports car regulations. It was a device heartily disliked by the drivers, who complained that it obscured their vision. Listers tried to counteract this by letting a section of glass into the Perspex, which can be seen clearly contained in the frame in front of the driver

body similar to that of XPE 2, eventually selling HWM 1 to hillclimber Ray Feilding. Then tragedy struck. Heath, whose bravery knew no bounds but whose driving skill was not quite in the Abecassis class, died when his HWM overturned in the Mille Miglia. The newly-wed Abecassis retired and HWM built only one more Jaguar-engined racing car, an Alta-based machine with cycle wings for Scragg.

As this industry was reaching its climax on the Surrey borders, a new wave of Jaguar specials was being created in Cambridgeshire. One of the most successful special builders of the early nineteen-fifties had been John Tojeiro, who constructed Cooper-inspired cars, first of all in a shed at Little Gransden and then in slightly larger premises at nearby Royston. His early customers included local agricultural engineering chief Brian Lister, and his best design was based on Cliff Davis's Ferrari Barchetta-like Cooper-MG. This design was sold to AC in 1953 to become the Ace and eventually the Cobra. The car had a Bristol engine and the natural progression was Jaguar power, so when a wealthy farmer in the Whitehead mould, John Ogier, approached Tojeiro, he was all ready to go on a Jaguar special.

He followed his brief much closer than Cooper and produced an ultra-light, all coil-sprung machine in 1956 after experiments with a Jaguar engine in another, older, Tojeiro, which originally had used a Lea-Francis engine like that in the RGS and Connaughts. It was probably the lightest Jaguar special ever at fifteen and a half hundred-weight and possessed truly phenomenal speed although,

Walt Hansgen took a few weeks off from driving Cunningham's Lister-Jaguar in SCCA events and promptly won three out of the four races he entered in the works Lister-Jaguar, VPP 9, in Britain in 1958. Here he beats New Zealanders Ross Jensen and Bruce Halford's Lister-Jaguars into second and third places at Snetterton in July 1958. The number VPP 9 has been the subject of considerable controversy over the years. It is believed that the number was carried on three or four Lister-Jaguars. The last one was crashed fatally by Roy Bloxham at Goodwood in 1961; parts of this Costin-bodied car are thought to have been sold to an Australian, and a Costin-bodied car has reappeared in Australia recently, bearing the legendary number. However, the same number has appeared on a "knobbly" bodied car raced by John Harper in British historic events, and he has the log-book, which matches its chassis number, BHL 3. This number comes from a very early Lister, probably a Bristol-engined example

Yet another example of the Costin-bodied Lister-Jaguar; this fixed-head coupé was raced in long-distance events by Peter Lumsden and Peter Sargent in 1963 and by John Coundley and Jack Fairman in 1964. This was the last Lister made, in 1959, and featured an experimental space frame, although, to add to the general confusion, it bore the registration number WTM 446. This number had been used on Coundley's normal open-bodied Costin car in 1960. The Coundley car was crashed later that year while making the Mille Miglia-based *Green Helmet* film, giving rise to yet another pile of "VPP 9" parts! The Costin coupé, pictured here before retirement in the 1964 Nurburgring 1000 kilometre race, was later rebodied in standard Costin form as Hexagon of Highgate's historic racer

with bodywork reminiscent of a D type, its suspension and braking lacked development. Nevertheless, Protheroe—Ogier found the car rather too quick for himself—had considerable success in this machine, registered 7 GNO, against works Maseratis, Astons and Jaguars in 1956. A sister car was built in 1957, achieving similar success in the hands of drivers such as Jack Brabham, Jack Fairman and Graham Hill.

Meanwhile Lister had been building his own cars, powered, at first, by an MG engine in 1953, then by Bristol power in the latter half of 1954 and 1955, and finally a 2-litre Maserati engine for 1956. They were by far the fastest specials on British circuits, but although the Maserati engine proved highly unreliable, Lister had shown little interest in Jaguar power as his eyes were set on Formula Two for his star driver, Archie Scott-Brown.

However, hillclimbing jeweller Norman Hillwood fitted a C type Jaguar engine into a Lister-Bristol chassis early in 1957 and promptly showed everybody else the way to go. At the same time, the Shell-backed Jaguar team had withdrawn from racing and through their BP association were able to persuade Lister to build a Jaguar-engined car. He had little option since much of his finance came from BP. Lyons was only too happy to supply a really potent dry sump D type engine and transmission, and in Scott-Brown's hands the works Lister-Jaguar became the top car on

above
The one and only single-seater Lister-Jaguar, the "Monzanapolis", in practice for the 1958 Italian event, with Jack Fairman at the wheel. It was fitted with large seventeen-inch wire wheels at the rear in an attempt to minimize the tyre trouble that had struck the D type Jaguars in 1957; alloy disc wheels like those at the front could not be used as they were not available in sizes of more than sixteen inches. The seventeen-inch wheels helped to give the Monzanapolis Lister-Jaguar a nose-down attitude, combating the cars' well-known tendencies to lift at high speed. However, in the event, the drag of the exposed wheels slowed the car too much to be competitive

left
The Monzanapolis Lister, which had been intended eventually for Indianapolis, was sold to Phil Scragg for hillclimbing. He modified it to two-seater, cycle-wing road-going form, and registered it 254 KTU. It is pictured here at Shelsley Walsh in 1960. Several years later, after Scragg's death, the car was rebuilt to its original Monza trim to race in historic events. Alongside, the SS100 Old Number Seven, and one or two ex-Formula Two HWMs, it is one of the few open-wheeled Jaguar racing cars

Gordon Parker campaigned first his Jaguette, then his Jaguara, with great success until 1958, when he built the fearsome HK Jaguar. It had a relatively simple two-channel tubular chassis with coil spring suspension all round and de Dion tube at the rear. With a highly supercharged 3.4-litre XK engine, it proved fantastically fast in the dry but a veritable monster in the wet! Eventually Parker achieved his ambition of fastest time of the day at Brighton, in 1961. He is pictured here in the HK Jaguar at the start of his run at the highly disorganized 1962 meeting, in which he failed to get into the top dozen—but the HK Jaguar was quite successful later in the nineteen-sixties in the hands of Anthony Charnock

British circuits. It bore the famous registration number MVE 303, carried earlier on the all-conquering works Lister-Bristol.

There was nothing in quite the same class. Its roadholding was far superior to that of the Tojeiros (which had slightly less power for the same weight), its brakes were as good as those on the Coopers, traction was even better than that of the HWMs, and it had less weight than the works Jaguars, Aston Martins, Ferraris and Maseratis, which were built specifically for long-distance racing. To top it all, there were few drivers in the same league as Scott-Brown, despite his handicaps. Only Salvadori in the latest DBR2 Aston Martin could beat Scott-Brown on the ultra-high-speed Silverstone circuit, where the Lister's functional but "knobbly" body was not ideal. In 1957, Scott-Brown won twelve out of fourteen races entered, with a fastest lap on the one in which he retired.

Tojeiro built a new 7 GNO, selling the old one to Frank Cantwell in New Zealand, but both were written off around the end of 1957. Scott-Brown took MVE 303 to New Zealand and managed to beat Ross Jensen's Maserati 250F grand prix car for the Lady Wigram Trophy as Brian Lister was snowed under with orders. Most of his chassis were destined for America to be fitted with Chevrolet V8 engines, although Briggs Cunningham had two with D type engines to replace his Jaguars. In Walt Hansgen's hands they did a Scott-Brown, running away with the SCCA championships in 1958 and 1959.

One of Jaguar's most ambitious competitors in the early nineteen-fifties was Tommy Sopwith, of Hawker Aviation, who built the Sphynx sports car around the firm's Armstrong Siddeley car components. It was an attempt to show that their saloon cars were as good as the Mark VIIs, which had benefited from Jaguars racing successes to the extent that they were demolishing Armstrong Siddeley's traditional market. The Sphynx with its then fashionable Armstrong Siddeley pre-selector gearbox was reasonably competitive at first. The idea of the pre-selector was that it left both arms free to saw away at the steering wheel in hectic cornering! The Sphynx was also notable in that it used an Allard JR chassis, the culmination of Sydney Allard's attempts to stay ahead of Jaguars in the sports car field. By 1956, the Sphynx had been outclassed by the C and D types, so Sopwith bought a Cooper-Jaguar, then eventually gave in, and raced Jaguars . . . but the Sphynx lingered on and reappeared in Brian Croot's hands in historic and modified sports car racing in the late nineteen-sixties. It proved to be surprisingly competitive, partly because he had fitted it with a Jaguar engine! However, it was eventually refused entry to historic racing because it had departed too far from the original. Here it leads eventual winner Mike McGrath in the all-independently sprung D type at Snetterton in 1969

During 1958, Lister also ran a second works car, registered VPP 9, for Scott-Brown. This was a rebuild of an old Bristol-engined car to similar specification to MVE 303. His closest rival at the start of 1958 was Masten Gregory in another Lister-Jaguar belonging to the Ecurie Ecosse. They were racing neck and neck at Spa when tragedy struck. Scott-Brown hit one of the Belgian circuit's notorious damp patches—it can be dry in some places on the circuit and wet in other, unexpected, places—and overturned VPP 9 in flames. He died the next day . . . but Brian Lister was persuaded to carry on, against his will.

Stirling Moss, Ivor Bueb, Ross Jensen, Bruce McLaren and Walt Hansgen drove rebuilt cars registered VPP 9 with success and Jack Fairman drove an open-wheeled Lister-Jaguar in the second Monzanapolis race. However, the drag from its exposed wheels proved too much and it was slower than the 1957 D types. Later the car was sold to Scragg to have cycle-type wings fitted for hillclimbing.

top
Doug Alton in the Dalro-Jaguar holds off Ian Cummins's C type through Energol Corner for third place at Oran Park, Sydney, in June 1970. The Dalro was a total rebuild of the earlier Austral-Union, which in turn had been constructed from a crashed XK120 Roadster

above
One of the few open-wheeled Jaguar-engined racing cars is the Alta-Jaguar, pictured here at Silverstone in a historic event. This car is an adaptation of an early Alta Grand Prix car, like those used as the basis of the HWMs

The Alton-Jaguar pictured here in its home territory, the Jaguar Driver's Club Blackbushe airfield sprint, gave a lot of fun to its constructor, Mike Barker. He started building this pretty little special in 1954 around a supercharged two-litre Alta engine, but when this proved unreliable, he substituted a C type Jaguar engine and gearbox. The frame was the traditional special's twin-tubular ladder with Lotus-like coil spring front suspension and Aston Martin coil spring rear. With more than 200 bhp to propel its eighteen hundredweight (it had a Mistral glass-fibre body), the Alton-Jaguar proved highly competitive for years

The Ecurie Ecosse also equipped themselves with a new Tojeiro-Jaguar, again registered 7 GNO. It raced alongside their Lister and surviving D type with only marginal success—although Flockhart managed to win at Goodwood on Whit Monday in 1959.

The 1959 Listers were bulbous affairs, fitted with aerodynamic coachwork designed by Frank Costin; they were intended for long-distance racing and were slightly slipperier at high speed. The bulky body was something of a handicap, however, on close circuits and they were no faster than the earlier "knobbly" bodied cars in most competitions.

Tojeiro produced another car for the Ecurie Ecosse fitted with a 3-litre Jaguar engine, but it suffered from the usual problems associated with that power unit, then ran out of brakes; it was written off by Gregory in the TT at Goodwood in 1959. The Ecurie Ecosse's surviving Tojeiro was campaigned with their Lister in long-distance racing, and driven in some South African events with Tony Maggs at the wheel, before being sold to David Lewis for sprinting.

Like the D types, the Listers, Tojeiros, HWMs and Coopers were competitive cars with 3.4-litre or 3.8-litre engines; but they fell behind or failed to finish in long-distance events with the 3-litre unit. Their star was on the wane by 1960, although the Listers—always the fastest—continued to win club events in 3.8-litre form right into the mid-nineteen-sixties; the last Lister-Jaguar to run in a top long-distance event was the last made, an experimental space-framed car built in 1959, which competed at Le Mans in 1963 with an alloy E type engine. Sadly, it suffered from clutch trouble and its enthusiastic crew of Peter Sargent and Peter Lumsden had to retire. Vivienne Lewis won her class in the surviving Tojeiro-Jaguar at Brighton in 1961, then died two years later in a horrific crash while attempting to repeat the feat.

Practically all the HWMs and many of the Listers survived the club races of the early nineteen-sixties and provided a backbone for the historic sports car racing introduced by the Griffith Formula in 1966. Once again the Listers were to the fore, with strong competition from the occasional HWM, including the glorious old HWM 1. Many Listers were reimported from America without their original Chevrolet engines and rebuilt as Lister-Jaguars, with the result that there were more Lister-Jaguars racing than Brian Lister ever built! And so the Jaguar specials continue to dominate historic sports car racing today; they are ideal for this type of racing, which so closely corresponds to the club events of the nineteen-fifties in which they were at their best.

far right
Dr Phillipe Renault takes Mulsanne in the 1973 Le Mans historic race with his early Lister-Jaguar, 673 LMK. This Parisian dentist must rank as the world's greatest Jaguar collector, with more than fifty historic Jaguars in his collection. He is no Schlumpf, however. He does his best to have them all raced from time to time!

right
Typical historic sports car line-up at Silverstone with the Hexagon space-framed Costin Lister driven by Nick Faure next to Harper's "knobbly", with Anthony Hutton on the outside of the front row in 673 LMK. Behind him is the highly successful "knobbly" of David Ham, with yet another "knobbly" completing the second row!

UNLOP
BOSCH
673
LMK
104

DAILY EXPRESS
FROM START TO FINISH — ALWAYS IN THE LEAD
itax Britax
117
119
CAMEL HEXAGON
FILTERS
113

213
RALLYE MONTE-CARLO
ZJ 8726

Chapter 6
Grace, space, pace

Cecil Vard did wonders in the Monte Carlo Rally in Mark V saloons, finishing third in 1951 and fifth in 1953; he also took twenty-seventh place in 1955 with a Mark VII saloon. He is pictured here at a control on the way from Glasgow in the 1951 rally, in which he came within an ace of snatching victory from the eventual winner, Jean Trevaux, in a $4\frac{1}{2}$-litre Delahaye

Jaguar saloons have always been very fast, if somewhat bulky, for competition; but even the stately Mark V enjoyed a fair measure of success in the Monte Carlo Rallies of the early nineteen-fifties. And the Mark VII that followed actually won the Monte and dominated touring car races until the slimmer, more agile, Marks 1 and 2 took over to win everything going from 1957 to 1962. Even when huge American cars muscled in on saloon car racing in 1963, the Jaguar saloons had a future: they burned everything else off the track as soon as Classic saloon car racing started in 1975.

A Dubliner called Cecil Vard blazed the glory trail for Jaguars in 1951 when he finished third in the Monte Carlo Rally in his virtually standard Mark V saloon. In fact, he nearly won this historic rally, losing by less than a mark to a $4\frac{1}{2}$-litre Delahaye driven by Jean Trevaux, a car which cost twice as much and looked no better. Vard and co-driver Young had a pretty tough time on the way down to the Riviera from Glasgow with the rest of the British contingent. It was snow storms and slush all the way with one Citroën buried in an avalanche after they crossed the Channel; the chief opposition came from all-round ace Ken Wharton in a Ford V8 Pilot, starting an inter-marque rivalry that was to last a decade or more. On this occasion, Vard was backed by trials champion Walter Waring, ninth with W. H. Wadham in another Mark V. Reggie Tongue and Peter Warr took thirty-first place for Jaguar.

Even more snow fell in 1952, but it could not stop the Mark V's successor, the Mark VII. Cotton/Didier and Heurtaux/Crespin ploughed through it all to take fourth and sixth places in the Monte, although, in some ways, Ford had the last laugh that year. Sydney Allard won with a Ford V8-engined car of his own making. However, Allard was relegated to third place when Moss hit the track with a works Mark VII for the Silverstone Production Car race in 1952—the event the XK had dominated when sports cars were allowed to enter. Moss's Mark VII really captured the

Sydney Allard ploughed through terrible snow drifts to win the 1952 Monte Carlo Rally in one of his own saloons, as the Mark VII Jaguars of Walter Waring and Raymond Baxter fell victim of snowbound ditches. But the French Jaguar drivers were not deterred. R. Cotton/L. Didier and J. Heurtaux/M. Crespin took fourth and sixth places. Cotton and Didier are pictured here on a Riviera road running with snow water

crowd's heart as it rocked and rolled along, easily beating Wharton's Healey into second place. These racing Mark VIIs were relatively standard cars, with little attention being paid to stiffening the suspension or saving much weight. Their engines were tuned to produce about 210 bhp, however, and they were fitted with bucket seats—reckoned to be worth at least a second a lap!

Dutchman Maurice Gatsonides won the 1953 Monte with a works Ford Zephyr from Appleyard's Mark VII with Vard back with his old Mark V to take fifth place. He had experimented with a Lagonda the year before. Jaguars did very well really, with Air Vice-Marshal "Pathfinder" Bennett and his wife in eighth position in another Mark VII. These were almost standard cars, Appleyard's being modified only in that it was fitted with twin stopwatches and ballast to make up for Pat Appleyard's light weight! Generally, the Mark VIIs were used only when it was likely that the weather would be very bad; XKs were the favourite cars for normal rallies, although Denis Scott enjoyed some success in his father's everyday Mark VII. He said he just wanted to borrow it for the weekend, then won his class in the RAC Rally—to mutual paternal-filial satisfaction. And soon after he repeated the trick in the Morecambe Rally. . . .

Moss also did a repeat trick in the 1953 Silverstone Production Car race, easily outpacing Grace's 2½-litre Riley RM, which might have been highly placed the previous year had it not been for a collision. It really was becoming a matter of honour that Jaguars won this event each year—especially as it was assuming great importance in the public eye, and Mark VIIs were the mainstay of production.

Grand Prix driver Louis Chiron won the 1954 Monte, but Ulsterman Ronnie Adams was the talk of the Principality, such was his handling of his cumbersome Mark VII. Adams and co-driver Desmond Titterington were leading the field after the Gap-Monaco speed test with only a lap of the Monaco Grand Prix circuit to follow; but all the cards were stacked in the Monégasque's favour: he knew every inch of the circuit and he was driving one of the best-handling cars in the world, a Lancia Aurelia GT. Also, he had a handicap advantage in that his highly tuned engine displaced only 2.5 litres! However, Adams drove like a man possessed to lap in an incredible 2 minutes 24.6 seconds, only three seconds slower than Chiron—a seemingly impossible feat that earned him sixth place; two in front of Vard and Arthur Jolley in another Jaguar.

Once more the Mark VIIs won the Silverstone Production Car race, with Appleyard, Rolt and Moss in line-ahead formation, and, to emphasize their point, they all broke the previous lap record; Moss—who had been delayed with starting trouble—left it at 77.48 mph. In 1955 Hawthorn put it up to 81.06 mph in a similar car. Similar except that they had light alloy body panels, part of a batch that went to make a special magnesium-bodied Mark VII that had been intended for the 1954 race but never made it.

Stirling Moss leads the sprinters in his speciality—a Le Mans-style start—at the 1954 Silverstone Production Car Race. He had high hopes of a hat-trick in the event, having won in LWK 343 in 1952 and 1953. But this time the faithful Mark VII—which had also seen service with Raymond Baxter and Gordon Wilkins in the Monte Carlo Rally—jammed its starter; Moss had to rock it free, then storm through the field to take third place behind winner Ian Appleyard (second in the line-up with SUM 7) and second-place man Tony Rolt in the third works Mark VII, bearing race number five. Their chief rivals were the Daimler Conquest team led by Ken Wharton's car (race number twelve), Reg Parnell (his car is obscured behind Moss's helmet) and George Abecassis, plus Ronnie Adams's private Mark VII, registered OZ 5499 (race number two). Next to Adams's Jaguar are the 2½-litre Rileys of Lyndon Sims—who led the first lap!—and Harold Grace. Immediately behind the Rileys are Tony Crook's very fast Lancia Aurelia GT, which collided with Wharton's Daimler, eliminating both. Gerry Dunham's Alvis and Bert Rogers's Riley complete the cars visible in this historic picture

LWK 343 storms on to win the 1955 Silverstone production car race in the hands of Mike Hawthorn. Ian Stewart was second and Desmond Titterington third in other works Mark VIIs with Wharton fourth in a Ford Zephyr. Appleyard retired with water pump failure in SUM 7. Despite their ungainly appearance, the Mark VIIs lapped at the same speed as the fleet Formula Three racing cars!

It was a great year in 1955 for the Mark VII. It won the team award in the production car event with Ian Stewart and Titterington backing up Hawthorn in second and third places; the team award in the Monte with Adams and Ernest McMillen eighth; Vard and Jolley twenty-seventh and Mattock and Page thirty-seventh, despite atrocious conditions in the Alps. Mark VIIs were frequently rallied, although the XKs were by far the more popular Jaguar competition machine—nevertheless R. B. Cade won the over 2600 cc class in the MCC Rally and on the track I. M. Gillett beat a 1900 Alfa Romeo and a Healey Silverstone to win the Goodwood saloon handicap. The mind boggles to think what sort of saloon the Healey Silverstone was, although anything with a hard top was allowed into these races in those days. Aston Martins even advertised their two-seater DB2 as a saloon!

If 1955 was a good year for the Mark VII in rallying, 1956 had to be the greatest. Ronnie Adams actually won the Monte Carlo Rally in his works machine—the only car of more than 2500 cc to finish in the first thirty-eight! The performance of Adams and his crew of Derek Johnston and Frank Biggar on the Paris–Monaco and the Mountain Circuit stages was a marvel of consistency—and they even returned the second best time in the braking test with a car totally unsuited for such tortuous manoeuvres. Later,

Ronnie Adams receives garlands and accolades outside the Palace at Monte Carlo after his historic rally win of 1956

when John Bolster tested the car for *Autosport*, he ran into a blizzard just like those encountered by Adams in the Alps. "As the drifts got larger and larger, I felt that there was no hope of turning back, and I pressed on hard in second gear, while the screaming wind covered my tracks almost as soon as I had passed. The sheer weight of the car, once it was really in motion, carried it through drifts that would have stopped even some four-wheel-drive vehicles," said Bolster of the thirty-four-hundredweight beast that had already seen two Montes and a Silverstone race.

It was a significant year, too, in that it marked the introduction of the first of the small Jaguar saloon racers, the 2.4-litre Mark 1. Frank Grounds gave the model its first outing, and success, in the RAC Rally, winning the under 2700 cc class and finishing fourth overall; the principal competition came from works Austin A90s and Ford Zephyrs—but the Press were convinced that the Jaguar had them all beaten: they called it the "Best All Round car on the market today." The title was justified, for in May Paul Frère won the eighty-eight-mile Spa production car race with Ninian Sanderson in a D type winning the main event.

Hawthorn howls round Copse in his works 3.4-litre Mark 1 saloon not much more than a length ahead of Archie Scott-Brown's similar Jaguar in the 1957 Silverstone Production Car Race. Scott-Brown's brakes gave up after five laps, leaving second place to Duncan Hamilton's 3.4 Mark 1 with another driven by Ivor Bueb in third position

Jaguars picked a mixed bunch for the 1956 Silverstone Production race: Mark VIIs for Ivor Bueb and Frère; 2.4s for Hawthorn and Duncan Hamilton. Hawthorn howled into the lead only to drop a valve and retire after the first couple of laps; this let Bueb into the lead, with Wharton taking second place in his Austin A90 Westminster. Hamilton fought his way through to third with Frère fourth, so Jaguars had covered themselves in glory again. The Westminster, by the way, was fitted with an Austin-Healey engine, Weber carburetters and lowered, stiffened, suspension; racing saloons were getting more like racing cars every day.

Jaguars replied in the most obvious manner by dropping their 3.4-litre engine into the Mark 1 in 1957 to effectively demolish all opposition for years to come. In the meantime, Arthur Knight sprinted his private 2.4, bearing a registration number that was later to become famous—BUY 1—as the factory prepared 3.4s for the Production Car Race at Silverstone. "My word, how they go," said Gregor Grant in *Autosport*. "Mike Hawthorn's winning race average this year was 82.19 mph, which beats last year's

94
RALLYE MONTE-CARLO
ULU 333
94

Three-point-four Mark 1 Jaguars distinguished themselves in the 1959 Monte Carlo Rally with Bobby Parkes and George Howarth winning their class and finishing eighth overall. Ninth was Walton and Martin's similar car, which, with Brinkman and Cuff, backed up Parkes and Howarth to win the much-prized Charles Faroux team award. Other British-entered Jaguars were not so lucky; Eric Haddon and Norman MacLeod, pictured here between Luc and Lanaogne, were eliminated in the final stages

fastest lap, set up at 81.68 mph by Ivor Bueb in a Mark VII. This time the intrepid conductors of the four fastest machines were Hawthorn, Bueb, Hamilton and Archie Scott-Brown, and they hurled the cars around the bends for all they were worth, the door-handles nearly scraping the ground. The whole process was quite horrifying, the new cars appearing to be even more flexibly sprung than the Mark VII." Flexibly sprung or not, Hawthorn won from Hamilton and Bueb after Scott-Brown had to yield second place due to brake trouble. Like the Fords and Austins, these cars were well modified. "There were heavy anti-roll bars front and rear, the back shock absorbers were special, an extra leaf was added to each of the rear springs, and a Powr-Lok limited slip differential was fitted. The engine was a normal 3.4-litre modified as follows: a C type head with

Black ice and frozen snow decimated the field in the 1959 Monte Carlo Rally, but the German crew of Lindner/Walter were well equipped. Their 3.4-litre Mark 1 Jaguar had Trelleborg tyres fitted with metal-ring inserts, carrying two spares on the roof. They are pictured here storming an Alpine gorge before being eliminated like Haddon and Norman. Citroëns from Paris finished in the first four places

high-lift camshafts and two 2-inch SU carburetters, 9:1 compression ratio and lead bronze bearings. A racing clutch transmitted the power through a close-ratio gearbox to a 3.54 axle. The overdrive was locked out for racing. The battery was placed in the boot to improve weight distribution and racing tyres were fitted. The exhaust system was standard save that twin straight-through silencers reduced back pressure slightly," said Hamilton in his autobiography *Touch Wood!* Hawthorn's car was identical, and tragically the one he was to die in after a crash on the Guildford by-pass in 1959.

Meanwhile the factory were preparing a 3.4 for da Silva Ramos to drive in the Tour de France—a sort of rally for racing drivers with a series of hillclimbs and circuit races all over the country. Da Silva Ramos made the fastest time on

Donald Morley in car number sixty-one lines up with Eric Brinkman's 3.4 to do battle with Steunebrink's Chevrolet Impala at Zandvoort for the final stage of the 1959 Tulip Rally, won by the Morley twins. Donald won the Zandvoort race from Brinkman with the Chevvy wallowing in third

the early climb of La Turbie to lead the all-important touring category from the French rally champion Bernard Costen with co-driver Jack Renal. But Costen and Renal stormed through at the end in their private 3.4 for the first in a fantastic series of wins in this event.

The 3.4s were becoming more and more modified to great effect by 1958. Disc brakes helped reduce lap times for cars such as those driven by Tommy Sopwith and Sir Gawaine Baillie, who finished the 1957 season on Boxing Day at Brands Hatch as they continued all through 1958: first and second in the modified saloon car series, with all the others a mile or more behind. Sopwith even used his Equipe Endeavour car for rallying, pushing Peter Harper's Sunbeam Rapier hard in the 1958 RAC event. And a bright new team of twins, Don and Erle Morley, won their class in the Tulip Rally with a 2.4. As Sopwith and team-mate

Baillie mopped up overall wins and the unlimited class, Jack Sears won everything going in the under 2700 cc class with his ex-Wharton Austin A105. Sopwith was hardly ever beaten, and then only by the likes of Hawthorn in the Silverstone International Trophy meeting and Walt Hansgen on his racing holiday at the British Grand Prix supporting race. The result was that he tied for first place in the first British saloon car championship with Sears, but lost the title in a race-off: BMC supplied them both with Riley 1.5s and then they had two five-lap duels at Brands Hatch in alternate cars to decide the title! Sopwith didn't mind too much; he'd retired at the end of the season anyway and had had all the glory of winning the events outright. And his involvement in saloon car racing didn't end there: he continued as the outstandingly successful entrant of the Equipe Endeavour cars.

Jack Sears hammers into the lead in Tommy Sopwith's Equipe Endeavour 3.8-litre Mark 2 Jaguar in the touring car race supporting the British Grand Prix at Silverstone in 1960. Reflected in the highly polished side of the car is another 3.8-litre Mark 2 driven by Lotus car constructor Colin Chapman. Hard as Sears drove, he couldn't drop Chapman—making one of his last competitive appearances behind the wheel. After seven laps, Chapman squeezed past with Sears on the grass, then they swopped positions again and again in a furious duel before Chapman scraped by at Woodcote to win by 0.2 second on the last lap

The Jaguar 3.4s did well in the 1959 Monte, Bobby Parkes and George Howarth winning their class and taking eighth place overall with Walton and Martin ninth. Citroën won overall, but the Jaguars won the team award with Birkman and Cuff in thirty-seventh place. This was all just a prelude to something great in the rally world, however.

The Morley twins, with Bill Hercock as third man, bought a brand-new 3.4 and within a fortnight drove it to victory in the toughest-ever Tulip Rally! Appalling weather added to the hazards in the Alps and, when the ninety-three survivors reached Noodwijk Aan Zee, there were apparently only two crews with clean sheets. Owing to the scrubbing of a couple of time controls, the unpenalized number rose to five, a remarkably low number for a contemporary championship rally, surpassed only by the Liège-Rome-Liège, which, apart from Johnny Claes's classic drive in an XK120, finished with all competitors

One of the most amazing drivers of the late nineteen-fifties and early nineteen-sixties was Doc Shepherd, the Cambridge GP who took up motor racing at fifty-eight years old after injuring his back in a horse riding accident. He was sixty when he had his greatest season in 1960, his Weslake-modified Austin A40 prepared by Lister-Jaguar ace Don Moore frequently finishing second and third overall to the winning Jaguar in touring car races. In this picture, he is about to overtake Albert Powell's 3.4-litre Mark 1 going uphill at Brands Hatch to finish second overall behind Sears. Powell hung on grimly for third place in front of Peter Sargent's 3.4-litre Mark 1 and Bill Aston's similar car, pictured above chasing Shepherd. Later the flying doctor won at Snetterton from four Jaguars!

left
Roy Salvadori in the famous John Coombs 3.8-litre Mark 2, registered BUY 12 (for, Buy one, too!), leads Charles Kelsey's Chevrolet Chevvy II at Crystal Palace in June 1962. It was the start of the American invasion that was to overwhelm the Mark 2s the following year. In this race, the three Jaguars of Salvadori, Sears and Sir Gawaine Baillie occupied the front row of the grid with two Chevvy IIs on the second row. Kelsey powered his way into second place behind Salvadori by North Tower Crescent on the first lap, followed here by Sears in the Equipe Endeavour car with Baillie's private Jaguar fourth. Sears outmanoeuvred Kelsey for second place at South Tower corner on lap three, harassing Salvadori all the way after that. They crossed the finishing line with Salvadori in first place, Sears second, Kelsey third, with Baillie fourth. Kelsey, however, was disqualified for having an illegal exhaust system—with more development the big American cars would become a real menace to the all-conquering Jaguars

One of the most interesting races of the 1962 season from the historic point of view was the Oulton Park Trophy GT event in which a wide variety of contemporary cars competed, giving a good comparison of their relative performances. Innes Ireland started in pole position in a Ferrari 250 GT Berlinetta alongside Graham Hill in the Coombs E type, Mike Parkes in another 250 GT and Tony Maggs in the Essex Racing Stables Aston Martin DB4GT Zagato. Protheroe in the first of his E types was on the second row next to Mitchell's E type and Mike Salmon's Aston Martin DB4GT Zagato. Salvadori's 3.8-litre Mark 2, David Hobbs's E type, Pitt's Aston Martin DB4GT and Robin Sturgess's E type made up the third row. The fourth row comprised the Mark 2s of Sears and Dodd alongside Davenport's E type. Sir Gawaine Baillie's Mark 2 had Bob Olthoff in David Dixon's Austin-Healey 3000, registered DD 300, and Derrick Astle's similar Big Healey, plus Dick Crosfield's Daimler SP250 for company on the fifth row. The last row was made up of the old Aston Martin DB2/4 Drop-head of J. A. Wray-Roberts and Ferrari 250 GT of R. Cowles. Hill and Parkes beat Ireland off the line for Parkes to take the lead during the first lap before Ireland roared through into second place. By lap three the order resolved itself as Parkes, Ireland, Hill, Maggs, Hobbs, Salmon, Protheroe, Salvadori and Sears among the front runners. Then Hill broke the lap record, only for Parkes to respond by breaking it again. After six laps of the twenty-five-lap race, Astle, Cowles and Wray-Roberts had been lapped by Parkes, before the Aston Martin collided with Ireland as he was about to pass it five seconds later. The Aston retired battered and Ireland lost one and a half minutes having pieces of bodywork torn away and a wheel changed. Salvadori continued to lead Sears in the saloon car section and Olthoff in DD 300 stayed ahead of much more powerful machinery, including two E types. By lap twenty, Ireland had repeatedly broken the lap record to claw his way up to fourth place behind Parkes, Maggs and Hill—which is how the order stayed until the end. In the first picture Maggs is about to lap Salvadori. In the second picture, Sturgess's E type, race number ten, leads Pitt's Aston Martin DB4GT (registered 18 TVX), Baillie's Mark 2, Dodd's Mark 2, Olthoff's Big Healey, Crosfield's Daimler, Wray-Roberts and Cowles

FERC
18 TVX
GB 448
2 BBC

By August Bank Holiday 1963 the Jaguar Mark 2 no longer dominated saloon car racing—but continued to give a good account of itself. Here Graham Hill overtakes one of the hordes of Mini Coopers at Brands Hatch to take second place behind world champion-to-be Jim Clark in a Willment Ford Galaxie

penalized. Runners-up included Triumph, Ford, Porsche and Saab, and BMC were so impressed they signed up the Morley twins on the spot for their Austin-Healey team.

On the track, 1959 started with a furious duel between Bueb, Salvadori and Baillie in 3.4s and continued with Bueb doing most of the winning at speeds slightly faster than those of Sopwith the previous year. The Bristol car dealer won the Silverstone Production Car Race from Salvadori and Baillie, with two other 3.4s, driven by Protheroe and Tom Dickson, in fourth and fifth places and the class-winning 2.4 of Peter Blond sixth. As this furious onslaught on saloon car racing was raging south of the Mersey, Phil Walton was winning northern events in his 3.4 with Doug Uren's 3.4 engaged in desperate duels with Bernie Rodgers's Peerless GT in closed car club events.

The 3.4s of Walton and Pinder-Smith/Johnson were two of the few in the 1960 Monte—and were defeated by fuel problems and slippery surfaces as Mercedes-Benz took the first three places. However, Robert Gentilini and Paul Justamond won their class and were third on general classification in a 3.4 in the Lyons-Charbonnières Rally in March 1960.

April 1960 marked the competition debut of an even faster Jaguar, the Mark 2. The driver was Australian David McKay, who had enjoyed some success with a factory-

prepared 3.4 Mark 1, modified "from a prescription" by Jaguar service manager and former competitions manager Lofty England. When McKay visited Coventry to order his Jaguar, he told England what he wanted to do with it—use it on the road and race it in Australian saloon car events. England called in an aide, jotted some notes on a piece of paper, and said: "Have that done." Within a few days McKay drove away in his car with full works modifications other than that 8:1 pistons were fitted, "as Mr England did not consider that our petrol was good enough for the higher compression." He was, therefore, confident to order the first racing Mark 2, a 3.4-litre, and set off on a winning spree in the Tasman series supporting events, swopping first places with Ron Hodgson's 3.8 D type-engined Mark 1.

The fastest and most glamorous Mark 2, the 3.8, made its British debut in Baillie's hands, finishing third behind Sears's Aston Martin DB4 and Protheroe's 3.8 XK at Aintree in May 1960, although Baillie was soon on the winning trail at Oulton Park later that month. In lesser events, ex-Vickers test pilot Bill Aston, who had bought Baillie's old 3.4 Mark 1, finished second behind Albert Powell's 3.8 with Vic Parness's 3.8 at Brands Hatch before moving into the big time.

In European rallying, John Boardman and Whitworth won their class in the Tulip with a 3.8 Mark 2, backed by

Racing Jaguar saloons enjoyed a varied life during the nineteen-sixties. Here John Sparrow fights it out with an assortment of machinery, including a works Mini Cooper, Lancia Flaviasport Zagato, a BMW and a Lotus Cortina, at Brands Hatch. His car, 1628 VC, started life on 24 October, 1960, "to be run to destruction by the factory's experimental department" Salvadori drove it on many occasions before this much-modified 3.8-litre Mark 2 was sold to Sparrow, who campaigned it with considerable success until 1965. During this time it took numerous awards, including class wins in the Nurburgring Twelve Hour in 1964 and the European Touring Car championship at Zandvoort. Later the car is believed to have been used for drag racing and wound up with a 7-litre Chevrolet engine—but it is now being restored to original to race again. It takes a lot to run a Mark 2 to destruction . . .

Bobby Parkes and Gatsonides in similar cars. On the track, Peter Sargent took over the ex-Coombs 3.4 Mark I that had been driven by Salvadori, enjoying considerable success in club events. This car was one of the ultimate Mark Is, with 10:1 compression ratio engine, oversize valves, triple 2-inch SU carburetters, big sump, racing clutch, close ratio gearbox, overdrive, 3.77:1 rear axle, Powr-Lok differential, stiffened suspension, modified camber, wide rear track, disc brakes all round, straight-through exhaust, bucket seats, alloy doors, bootlid and bonnet (although a standard steel door was retained on the driver's side for safety). The early 3.8 Mark 2s were modified in similar vein except that their shells were strengthened even more around the rear axle location points, and the high ratio Mark I steering box substituted for the lower ratio standard Mark 2 box.

Salvadori was on top form in Jaguar's Surrey distributor John Coombs's new 3.8 Mark 2 for the International Trophy race at Silverstone in May, beating Moss in the Equipe Endeavour car, Graham Hill in the Team Speedwell 3.8, and Baillie, in that order. These races were really thrilling, with the Jaguars miles out in front, Leston's Volvo sometimes vanquishing the Zephyrs and the spectacular new Minis cornering sideways with smoke

Jaguar saloons turned up in club events throughout the late nineteen-sixties. Here B. E. Rutland brakes for the chicane at Goodwood in April 1966. The photographer was Paul Skilleter, on trial for his first job in motoring journalism, on *Motor* magazine.

pouring from their tyres. Tyres were quite a problem with the Jaguars, too, lasting little more than a dozen laps.

Drivers changed from race to race, with Lotus chief Colin Chapman starring in the British Grand Prix meeting's touring car race at Silverstone. "With four 3.8 Jaguars on the front row, the start was as noisy and as impressive as any Grand Prix," said *Autosport*, "and it was Sir Gawaine Baillie who took an initial lead. But at Stowe, Jack Sears was in front, followed by Colin Chapman, Sir Gawaine Baillie, Bill Aston in a 3.4 Jaguar and Dennis Taylor's 3.8.

"At the end of the first lap it was still Sears in the lead, coming through Woodcote in a full-bore drift that nearly got out of hand. Then came Chapman, Baillie, Aston, Taylor, Kennerley (3.4), Alan Hutcheson, leading the 1600 cc class in his Riley 1.5, Hopkirk (Rapier), Peter Harper (Rapier), Leston (Volvo), Bill Blydenstein (Borgward), Jeff Uren (Zephyr), Haynes (Zephyr), and, closely engaged, Doc Shepherd and Nickey Byrne, fighting for the lead in the 1000 cc class."

Chapman eventually forced his way through to win with the rest of the field driving like they were in a high-speed stock car race, all the way down the line to Shepherd, whose A40 beat Byrne's Auto Union by 0.8 second from Aley's Mini.

By 1966, there was hardly a Jaguar to be seen in international touring car races. Works BMWs were trouncing Alfa Romeo GTAs with opposition from Lotus Cortinas and Ford Mustangs. In the Spa Twenty-Four Hour Race, Hubert Hahne and Jackie Ickx in a BMW 2000TI beat the GTAs of Pinto/Demoulin and Gosselin/Pilette with all manner of cars behind. In among them all, in fifth place overall, was the 3.8-litre Mark 2 of Frenchmen Robert Dutoit and Eddy Meert. They were second in class, despite a considerable delay with a broken oil pipe, to a 4.7-litre Ford Mustang

This sort of thing went on all season with one warning sign in the Silverstone Production Car event. Jaguars had won it ever since it started and the crowds were anxious to see somebody else giving them some competition. It came in the form of Dan Gurney's all-American giant, a Chevrolet Impala. He took pole position beside Hill, Salvadori and Mike Parkes, who had been having spectacular success all season with his Equipe Endeavour car. Gurney powered into the lead, leaving the Jaguars trailing, until one of his wheels collapsed. These American heavyweights had oodles of power but lacked development for British circuits.

Jaguars won the race, of course, by default, with hard-driving Hill first, Parkes second and Bruce McLaren third.

In the Alpine Rally, José Behra/Richaud and Bobby Parkes/Howarth both won coupés, and in the Tour de France, Consten and Renal won yet again, by a small margin from the Baillie/Jopp 3.8. In the Monte Carlo

Long after its glory days in international racing, BUY 12 was campaigned in club events by London motor trader Tony Strawson. Here he leads John "Plastic" Pearson's XK120 in the Jaguar Drivers' Club Thruxton meeting in 1970. There was little to identify the grey car of old, only the registration number on the luggage boot. But that was the early nineteen-seventies . . .

Rally, foul weather and favourable handicapping gave the Panhards first, second and third places, with Walton and Birkman's 3.8s floundering, although Walton had the consolation of a hillclimb win. In sunnier climes Ian Geohegan, Hodgson, Bill Pitt and Ross Jensen starred in Jaguar saloons in the Tasman supporting events, and so it went on. . . .

Peter Berry Racing bought two 3.8s for McLaren and Dennis Taylor, with John Surtees standing in on occasions for McLaren. Salvadori in the Coombs 3.8 emerged as the star of most of the clashes with Sears, Parkes, McLaren, Taylor, Powell and Aston. Chris Kerrison drove a 2.4 Mark 2 with some success in the smaller class. Baillie and Jopp also competed in major rallies such as the 1961 Alpine, in which they won their class with the Morley twins as overall winners in their works Austin-Healey. These 1961 cars, of which Salvadori's frequently looked the most stable, were

Jaguar saloons prepared by Albert Betts continued to be successful in club events throughout the early nineteen-seventies. Here Reg Palmer's Mark 1 finished third in class in the Silverstone Tricentrol meeting in July 1975 with a much-modified A40 for company. Shades of the battles of old between the Jaguars and Doc Shepherd

fitted with full-race E type engines, lightened flywheels, close-ratio gearboxes, overdrive, competition shock absorbers and springs, reinforced rear suspension mountings, alloy uprights, thick discs, alloy calipers, alloy panels, bucket seats and wire wheels wide enough to take 6.40 × 15 racing tyres at the back.

The 1962 Monte Carlo Rally, won by Carlsson's Saab, was pretty well disastrous for the Mark 2, Walton and Robson eventually ploughing through for 118th place, emphasizing that the rally scene was rapidly becoming a place for small front-wheel-drive cars. However, Larry Rodriguez Larretta and Jack Greene won the 500-mile Buenos Aires production car race during that winter with consummate ease from three Alfa Romeo GTs, if you consider that twenty-five wheel changes for worn-out tyres was a trifling matter. Tyre consumption was an old problem that afflicted the heavy Mark 2s, particularly in long-distance events such as the Tour de France. On the British circuits in 1962, Graham Hill and Salvadori signed on for Coombs, with the Equipe Endeavour cars being driven by Sears and Parkes with competition from David Hobbs and Baillie among others. Generally the Coombs cars were in front, with the notable exception of the British Grand Prix meeting, in which Australian Bob Jane led Parkes and Sears in the opening laps, weaving from side to

Mark 2 Jaguars still perform well in club events, too. Here Tony Williams wins the special saloon class at Thruxton in August 1975 in his Risca Garages car

side to hinder attempts at overtaking until he overdid it and spun, eventually to retire with overheating; however, he had the consolation of making the fastest lap. Parkes and Jimmy Blumer also won *The Motor* Six-Hour Race at Brands Hatch in October from the Germans Lindner and Nocker.

In the Tour de France, Consten protested that the works-prepared cars driven by Sears/Lego and Baillie/Jopp had 2-inch carburetters, whereas the seven private 3.8s were still on 1.75-inch carburetters—but his protest was overruled. Nevertheless, the French rally champion won yet again, after the "2-inch" cars were eliminated by crashes, and 3.8s took the first five places in the touring category.

The year 1963 started well for Jaguar saloons: Peter Sargent, John Beckaert, Geoff Duke, Peter Lumsden and Andrew Hedges broke four International Class C records with a standard 3.8 by driving 10,000 miles at an average speed of 106.58 mph through heavy rain and thick fog at Monza; and Salvadori signed on for magazine magnate Tommy Atkins, promptly winning the Snetterton touring car race in his 3.8.

Then Sears got Willment's 7-litre 400 bhp Ford Galaxie 500 going to demolish the Jaguar opposition, with Salvadori second, Dodd third and Pendleton fourth at Silverstone in May. Gradually this enormous car was made trackworthy to dominate a form of racing which had been Jaguar's since 1949, or at least the short-distance events. The 3.8 saloon of Salvadori and Denis Hulme won the Brands Hatch Six-Hour race from Lindner and Nocker when the Willment Galaxie was withdrawn in a row over its disc-brake conversion, and the drum-braked car of Alan Brown and Jack Brabham was eliminated with tyre troubles. In fact, Mike Salmon and Peter Sutcliffe finished first, but their 3.8 was disqualified for having too-large valves. Later the Galaxie disc ban was confirmed, but they still kept winning short-distance touring car races. However, Lindner and Nocker won the Nurburgring Twelve-Hour race in their 3.8 in July 1963, and Nocker and privateers such as John Sparrow in an ex-works development car that had been driven by Salvadori, and Chris McLaren, had some success during the rest of the year; but really the writing was on the wall for the Mark 2—Galaxies were quicker in British touring car races.

Consten won the Tour de France yet again in a 3.8 from a similar car driven by two French ladies, Soisbault and Louisette, with Paddy Hopkirk and Henry Liddon third in a Mini Cooper S; suddenly new challengers were appearing everywhere for the Jaguars. Mercedes-Benz tried hard to win the European Touring Car championship with their 300SE, but Nocker's 3.8 was too good.

Sparrow and Nocker soldiered on in 1964, winning or taking places in a variety of European events as late as 1965—when the Mark 2s all but disappeared from the circuits in the face of the V8 onslaught. They starred from time to time in minor club events, even in drag racing, with other ancient Jaguars, until Classic saloon car racing started in 1975.

This was conceived as yet another attempt at a poor man's racing formula, for approved saloon cars made before 1957 plus others, such as the Mark IX Jaguar, in the spirit of the regulations. Modifications were limited and at first many of the cars were tatty and ill-prepared, but soon it became evident that there was nothing to touch a Jaguar, with the 2.4 Mark 1s winning everything and with an ultra-fast Mark VII driven by Graig Hinton providing much of the entertainment. By 1978, the RAC had stepped in with a firm hand, insisting on full roll cages to the detriment of interior trim such as seats, effectively turning the cars into real racers—much to their amateur drivers' annoyance. They wanted to keep them as dual-purpose road cars, but it seems that progress overruled them. Nevertheless, while the regulations continue to exclude the latter-day V8s, the Jaguars will keep on winning this gloriously nostalgic form of racing with a spot of competition from their old rivals, the Ford Zephyrs.

Classic saloon car racing has been all the rage since 1975 with Jaguars, particularly those of Graig Hinton, well to the fore. Here Graig corners his cumbersome Mark VII in inimitable style, entering the chicane at Donington "with a touch of opposite lock". British understatement at its best . . .

Ken Baker in 7 CXW swings wide at Snetterton in March 1962 as he fights it out with David Hobbs's Mechamatic Lotus Elite (number 126) and Gordon Jones's Gullwing Marcos (135) behind eventual winner Sturgess. The roadster versions of the E type, such as 7 CXW, were far more popular in club racing in the early years, coupés being rarely seen

Chapter 7
E types are for ever

There will never be another sports car quite like the E type: the series production car based so closely on the great D type racing machine. To celebrate its immaculate ancestry, the E type won its first race only weeks after being announced in March 1961. Graham Hill in Sopwith's E type led home fellow Grand Prix star Innes Ireland in an Aston Martin DB4GT at Oulton Park with Salvadori third in Coombs's E type despite trouble with fuel surge. E types, particularly in the hands of Robin Sturgess and Ken Baker, continued to contest British club events fiercely, despite mounting opposition from lightweight Ferrari 250 GTs and Aston Martin DB4GTs—the British Ferraris. Gradually the very expensive and specialized Ferraris got the upper hand and there seemed no future for the near-standard E types in international racing when the world sports car championship was transferred to their GT class and Ferrari built the wonderful 250 GTO purely for this championship. The 265 bhp twenty-four hundredweight steel-bodied E types were no match for the 300 bhp twenty-one hundredweight Ferrari racing cars, and Cunningham and Fitch could only finish fourteenth at Sebring in 1962, while the Germans Werner and Olsen were six laps behind the winning Ferrari driven by Mike Parkes and Willy Mairesse in the Nurburgring 1000 kilometres.

Nevertheless, Cunningham soldiered on at Le Mans with Salvadori, and British privateers Peter Lumsden and Peter Sargent, Maurice Charles and John Coundley backed him up. The Lumsden/Sargent car went really well, challenging for third place until it suffered suspension maladies and dropped back to fifth at the end, with Cunningham's coupé moving up to fourth. A Ferrari prototype won, however, with 250 GTOs second and third. Cunningham continued to race his car with some success in America, while Jaguars started to do a spot of development on Coombs's car, now registered 4 WPD, the BUY 1 number having been transferred to his 3.8 saloon. Protheroe also forged to the front with a near-standard coupé, registered CUT 7.

Robin Sturgess's E type prepares to take Robin Stelfox's Triumph TR3 at Copse in the Silverstone Six-Hour Relay Race in 1961. The Jaguar Drivers' Club team in this handicap event were Maurice Charles (D type), Sturgess, Eric Brown (XK120), Don Smith (XK150S), Peter Sargent (3.4 Mark 1) and P. J. Woodroffe (3.4 Mark 2). They were in the lead when Sturgess was on the track thanks to a great start by Charles. However, the two fastest cars in any one team were allowed only 100 laps between them, so Brown had to take over from Sturgess after the rapid E type had covered only thirty laps; Brown hung on grimly as the lead slowly evaporated, the team eventually finishing third behind the winning Sebring Sprites (seventeen laps advantage over the Jaguars) and the second-placed Octagon Austin-Healeys (six laps advantage)

Extensive weight saving on 4 WPD removed about two hundredweight of surplus metal, while the engine's power was increased to D type standards. Still Salvadori could manage only fourth place in the 1962 Tourist Trophy race with Protheroe seventh in his heavier car. Ferrari GTOs won, of course, and Jaguars decided that something better ought to be done to assist their faithful supporters, even if they could not afford the time and effort needed to mount another major offensive as they had done in the nineteen-fifties.

So they built twelve lightweight E types for international racing, as less extensively modified cars, such as Baker's 7 CXW, continued to mop-up club events. These light-weights were quite something: they were all roadsters, right-hand-drive, with alloy monocoques, aluminium hard-tops and alloy-block fuel-injection 3.8-litre engines

good for 300 bhp or more. The suspension was beefed up to eliminate the standard cars' habit of wallowing, and D type wheels, with sturdier disc brakes and alloy calipers, further improved the handling and braking. Coombs's car was rebuilt as the first in this exclusive line (around chassis number S850060) with the second (S850659) for Cunningham, 0660 for US West Coast distributor Kjell Qvale, 0661 for Tommy Atkins, 0662 for German distributor Peter Lindner, 0663 for Lumsden, 0664 and 0665 for Cunningham, 0666 for Peter Sutcliffe, 0667 for Bob Jane, 0668 for Dick Wilkins and 0669 for Phil Scragg. Three more semi-lightweights were built using steel centre-sections, a left-hand-drive Fixed-head coupé (S898183) going to French enthusiast Pierre Bardinon, S850817 to Sir Robert Ropner, and a third, with the special Sayer low-drag coupé body, to Protheroe to replace his original CUT 7.

Cunningham entered three E types for Sebring in 1963: number one was his first lightweight, S850659, another was his older coupé, registered 1337 VC, and the third, a hardtop roadster, for himself and Fitch. Bruce McLaren and Walt Hansgen had the lightweight and Richards and Kimberley drove the Le Mans car. Ed Leslie and Frank Morrill completed the line-up of four Jaguars versus eleven Ferraris. The two lightweight Jaguars fought valiantly, finishing seventh and eighth as the leading non-Ferrari runners during the height of half a decade of Italian dominance. They also won their class, finishing ahead of Carroll Shelby's emergent AC Cobras. And, soon after, Hill in 4 WPD beat Salvadori's Cooper Monaco to win the Snetterton International, which opened the European season. The lightweights were on their way. . . .

Lindner opened his season to lead the first lap of the Nurburgring 1000 kilometres to the amazement of everybody, especially Ferrari, holding fourth place for a long while until he hit engine trouble. Lumsden and Sargent

Graham Hill in the first lightweight, by far the fastest E type in 1962 GT racing, pictured here finishing second behind Mike Parkes's 250 GT Ferrari at Oulton Park in April, with Tony Maggs third in the Essex Racing Stable's Aston Martin DB4GT Zagato. Hill was actually faster in practice with 1 minute 55.8 seconds to Parkes's 1 minute 56.6, and was later to show himself capable of leading the Ferraris in Coombs's E type

took over in fourth spot only to crash. But non-lightweight E types finished 1-2-3 in their class and the lightweight had already proved a threat to the Ferraris.

Cunningham took his Sebring lightweight to Le Mans with his two new lightweights, the three being registered 5114 WK, 5115 WK and 5116 WK for Hansgen and Pabst, Cunningham and Grossman, Richards and Salvadori. Hansgen had gearbox trouble and Salvadori crashed on spilt oil; then Grossman had a lesser accident while in seventh place and struggled on for ninth, the first six places being occupied, predictably, by Ferraris.

The lightweights were further improved by the use of five-speed ZF gearboxes and as much as 344 bhp was extracted from Lindner's car, 4868 WK, while it was modified to Sayer shape for Le Mans in 1964. Lumsden's car, 49 FXN, was also rebodied in similar style and Protheroe was only narrowly beaten at Rheims in 1963 by Abate's Ferrari—but the lightweight E type was nearing the end of an era in international racing. Front-engined

David Hobbs in the ex-Bruce McLaren E type holds off Protheroe in the first CUT 7 and Trevor Taylor's incredibly fast Team Elite Lotus Elite in the GT race at the Silverstone International meeting in May 1962. Hobbs had to retire on lap three with low oil pressure and Protheroe quit when his throttle linkage broke; Taylor set lap records as he won the 1000–2000 cc class to finish fifth overall behind Jim Clark's DB4GT Zagato, Hill in 4 WPD, Masten Gregory in a Ferrari 250 GTO and Parkes's winning 250GTO

Protheroe had better luck in the Aston Martin Owners' Club meeting at Silverstone in July 1962. He led all the way in the GT race to win from Salmon's DB4GT Zagato (number nine)

DUNLOP
DUNLOP
CUT 7

right
E types were racing everywhere in 1963. Here Mi Nogueira Pinto wins the Taga Cidade de Luanda in his Portuguese-registered roadster. Note the front brake air cooling scoops and additional cooling scoop in the lip of the bonnet

below
Kerrison's Ferrari 250 GT leads Lumsden's Le Mans E type (number twelve, right), Salvadori in Coombs's E type (number eleven, left), Taylor in the Elite (right) and Chris Lawrence's Morgan Plus 4 away from the line in the Tourist Trophy race at Goodwood in August 1962. Ferrari 250 GTOs finished 1-2-3 (Ireland, Graham Hill, Parkes) with Salvadori fourth and Protheroe's E type sixth. Lumsden retired with handling problems

cars that could be used on the road, such as the E type and the 250 GTO, were on the way out to be replaced by rear-engined monsters that were to eventually almost kill sports car racing, they bore so little resemblance to road cars.

In the United States, Hansgen and Richards campaigned well, and Merle Brennan in a Qvale E type won forty-one SCCA production car races between 1963 and 1964; Lindner put up some soul-stirring drives with Peter Nocker before dying in a fearful crash in the wet at Montlhèry in October 1964. Sutcliffe won the Grand Prix de Paris on the same track that year in his E type, registered YVH 210, and took third place in South Africa's Rand Nine Hour Race with Dickie Stoop, behind the inevitable Ferraris.

Meanwhile eighteen-year-old Roger Mac took over the original CUT 7 E type in 1963 to win all manner of British club events, as world champion-to-be Jackie Stewart had similar success with a near-standard E type north of the border. Mac progressed to the ex-Atkins lightweight, 86 PJ, that had been raced so extensively by Salvadori, to further

8

12
898 BYR
LUCAS
AVON TYRES

right
Noblet and Guichet are off the line first in their Ferrari 250 GTO in the 1963 Nurburgring 1000 kilometre race, but Peter Lindner was soon in the lead in his E type (alongside the Ferrari). He had received the car (registered 4868 WK) only three days earlier, but stayed ahead of the works prototype 250P Ferraris of Surtees and Scarfiotti for the entire first lap. The E type and the 250 GTO battled for the lead in the GT class and third overall, with Lindner faster than Noblet and Guichet faster than Lindner's co-driver, Peter Nocker. Eventually the Lindner E type's engine failed and Lumsden's lightweight, delivered only on the Monday before the race in May, inherited fourth place behind the three Ferraris. Soon after Lumsden lost it at Flugplatz, crashing out of the race to leave Therstappen/Ruthardt and Werner/Olsen as the highest place E types in sixteenth and eighteenth positions

far right
Salvadori in Tommy Atkins's lightweight E type speeds past Wing Commander W. A. MacKenzie's Turner-Ford in the 1963 Tourist Trophy race at Goodwood. "Salvo", whose car was using the new five-speed ZF gearbox, was the only driver who could stay on the same lap as the winning Ferrari 250 GTOs of Graham Hill and Mike Parkes. Fourth was Jack Sears in another five-speed E type, two laps down

enhance his reputation in 1964, as other club races were terrorized by Rob Beck's 7-litre Ford Galaxie-engined E type, called the Egal. Graham Hill continued to put in development miles on 4 WPD until Jaguars gave up in 1965 to concentrate on the XJ13.

"You would have needed wider wheels than it was possible to fit to an E type," said Hill—but clubmen continued to race with startling success on rims of no more than six inches. They even competed in rallies, Merrick entering the Monte Carlo in 1961 and Pinder and Polther finishing well down in the same event in 1963.

One of the most successful of these enthusiasts was Londoner John Quick, who bought his E type, WOO 11, secondhand in 1964. Within a month he was driving this Fixed-head coupé in the Tulip Rally with little more than a good service and the fitting of two big spotlights on the front bumpers. He suffered from the standard E type's curse, brake fade, but finished fourth in his class. The car was gradually improved with rebuilt engine and stiffer suspension to take places in rallies, races and sprints all over Europe in 1964 and 1965—an outstandingly successful clubman's car.

46
67

31
444RAR
86 PJ

DUN
DURÉE
MARTINI
MARTINI
16
16

The Salvadori/Richards lightweight E type leads two other British cars at Tetre Rouge during the 1963 Le Mans race: Bob Olthoff and Sir John Whitmore in the Austin-Healey Sprite (number forty-two) and Chris Lawrence and Spender in the Deep Sanderson. None of them finished. Salvadori crashed in a huge pile-up caused by McLaren's Aston Martin flooding the track with oil when its engine exploded; the Sprite also crashed and the Deep Sanderson was eliminated with engine trouble

Cunningham and Grossman had their E type up to seventh place at Le Mans in 1963 until Grossman crashed, wrecking the bonnet. The bonnet from E type number fourteen, that of Hansgen and Pabst, which had been eliminated with gearbox trouble, was lashed on with holes cut in it for access to the oil and water fillers. Grossman is pictured here nursing the car home into ninth place

On the race track, 7 CXW was much rebuilt to win lots of races for Rob Schroeder, and Jackie Oliver and Chris Craft achieved a rare success for the new 4.2-litre E type in the Guards 1000 kilometre race at Brands Hatch in 1965. They finished third after leading at one point—but generally the 4.2-litre was only rarely favoured, the 3.8-litre engine, sometimes bored out to as much as 4 litres, surviving far higher revs. Scragg had a good deal of success on the hills, winning his class in the Shelsley Walsh Jubilee meeting of 1965 from Jim Thomson's E type.

In 1966, Quick and Warren Pearce started a fierce duel in production sports car racing, Quick's coupé having been rebuilt as a track car, Pearce having built his car up from a 1962 write-off. Pearce's roadster won seventeen outright victories from thirty-five starts in 1966, with development continuing apace for the next four years as this brand of racing turned into modsports. Quick had similar success, their E types being on top until Pearson's plastic XK moved into the same class. Then it became a close thing, with other drivers, such as northerner Ted Worswick in his ex-Keith

Holland E type, catching up. Throughout this era of British club racing, the E types were progressively lightened with glass-fibre panels and fitted with wide alloy wheels to become faster than the lightweights had been, Pearce's car even having a ZF gearbox.

E types were racing all over the world, even in Bolivia. Dr Jorge Burgoa of La Paz won Brazil's most important road race—rejoicing in the title of the Gran Premio Nacional de Automovilismo Rene Barrientos Ortuno—a long-distance event over 1200 miles on roads as high as 14,000 feet on Christmas Eve 1966. It was an extraordinary event, run in four stages and comparable in some ways to Australia's first twenty-four-hour race, in which the XK and C type had starred. It was run in much the same atmosphere, with dust replacing the mud. A Buick Supersport won stage one of this Bolivian burn-up, with Shelby Mustangs first and second on stage two before the race really took to the hills. It was then that the good doctor's roadster really came into its element. Hood down and bonnet off for better cooling, he soared over the mountains of Santa Cruz, leaving the Buick

Peter Lumsden's lightweight E type leads K. Aitchinson in Entwistle's TVR-MG through the chicane at Goodwood in the 1963 Tourist Trophy race. Lumsden finished ninth and the TVR eighteenth

Frank Gardner in the Willment AC Cobra leads David Cunningham's ex-Protheroe E type (sprayed in US racing colours!) off the line in the Silverstone over-1600 cc GT and prototype race in April 1964, with Brian Hetreed's Aston and Jack Lambert's E type making up the front row. Sneaking into the picture in the middle is Baker in 7 CXW with Peter Clark on the outside right, at the back, in his Ferrari 250 GTO. Gardner won from Hetreed and Clark, with Rob Beck's XK fourth; definitely not an E type day!

and Shelby's wildlife eating his dust. It was all too much for the pride of America. They retired, leaving the lone E type to steam on to the finish, crossing the line with an aggregate of 19 hours 47 minutes 31.1 seconds and dust in every nook and cranny. It's true that Willy Zalles's Mustang finished second, but he was one and a half hours behind!

Back in England, the modsports E types entered their last good year in 1971 with John Harper driving the last really competitive car, a rebuild of the eternal 7 CXW. Practically the only part that remained of what had left the factory in 1961 after ten years' hammering round British circuits and numerous crashes was the chassis plate, screwed to the rear where a number plate ought to have been. Over the years, racing E types bearing this registration number were never driven on the road, but probably won more events than any other single Jaguar. What did it matter if

Autosport editorial assistant Patrick McNally found the ideal way to report the 1964 Nurburgring 1000 kilometre race—from the driving seat of an E type coupé. Here the near-standard car he shared with Warwick Banks leads one of the class-winning Alfa Romeo Giulia TZs round one of the Ring's numerous bends, the Wehrseifen. McNally and Banks drove steadily to lead the over 3000 cc GT class at one point as faster cars, such as Linder's lightweight E type and Coundley's spaceframe Lister-Jaguar, dropped out. In the end, the E type was virtually pipped at the post by Schlesser and Attwood in an AC Cobra, which had been suffering from electrical trouble

TOTAL
TOTAL
16
CUT 7

CUT 7

left
Protheroe's low-drag coupé hangs on grimly to Salvadori in the Atkins lightweight E type towards the end of the International GT race at Silverstone in May 1964. The monocoques of the two E types were substantially the same, but the new CUT 7 had a much longer bonnet and smaller top in unit with the body rather than in standard detachable shape as on the Atkins car. They finished the race in that order, fifth and sixth behind Graham Hill's Ferrari 250 GTO, Salmon's Aston Martin, Sears's AC Cobra and Piper's GTO.

above
The long low nose of the Protheroe coupé is shown to good effect in this picture taken at the Rheims Twelve-Hour race in 1964. Here the Protheroe/Coundley car leads the 1964 Ferrari GTO of Parkes and Scarfiotti with one of the seven Porsche 904s hard on their tail, and Ulf Norinder's earlier GTO close behind. Parkes went on to finish second behind Graham Hill and Bonnier in a 3.3-litre 250LM prototype Ferrari, with the low-drag coupé eighth and Sutcliffe's lightweight E type fourteenth; Jackie Stewart and Chris Amon in the Norinder GTO finished nineteenth

The controversial start to the GT race at the British Grand Prix meeting at Brands Hatch in 1964. The E types of Salvadori (86 PJ), Sutcliffe (in front of him) and Protheroe (CUT 7) bring up the rear as Jackie Stewart's E type (centre) chases two Ferraris and Jack Sears's AC Cobra. "Due to a muddle by the organizers, Sears started from the front row of the grid instead of the second row," Denis Jenkinson reported in *Motor Sport*. "Jackie Stewart led in the Coombs E type and just when Sears was getting the Willment Cobra all set to make an attack for the lead he was given the black flag by the RAC officials. This means that there is something wrong with the car or the driver has transgressed a racing rule and he must stop at the pits next time round. Sears did this, and as he stormed into the pits area an official told him there had been a mistake and he could rejoin the race. He was now well down the field and Stewart had an enormous lead, but Sears rejoined the race in a really big way. He used all the power of the Ford V8 engine, flung the car through the bends in a fantastic manner, and charged after the leader. The reason for the black flag was that the officials felt that it was, in effect, a question of jumping the start, even though it was not his fault. Normally he would be penalized by having one minute added to his race time, but this did not seem fair as he would not know about the penalization and might have been content to beat Stewart by only thirty seconds, to find out that he had lost the race after it was all over. This would have dissatisfied everybody, so instead it was decided to black-flag him into the pits, the time lost being a form of handicap, but leaving him a sporting chance of making up for it. He certainly did make up for it, and the sight of that great thundering Cobra charging round Brands Hatch and gobbling up the Jaguar's lead was electrifying. Well before the end of the twenty laps, Sears was in the lead and he went on to win, so that the decision by the RAC officials, although an unusual one, actually made the race more exciting than it would have been."

the monocoque was changed four or five times, the car had Can-Am brakes, more than 300 bhp, plastic tail, bonnet and top, and ten-inch-wide wheels? It was still good old 7 CXW!

By 1972, modsports had progressed further and further away from the old ideal of a cheap racing formula. Warren Pearce alone had spent more than £40,000 on his self-prepared car over the years, and only E types powered by very special, and expensive, 4.5-litre engines—such as that of Brian Murphy, the ex-Warren Pearce car—stood any chance in this ultra-competitive formula. With this in mind, a production sports car formula was inaugurated in Britain in 1973. Eligible cars were divided into price classes of up to £1200; up to £1750; up to £4500 and over £4500. The £3000 V12 E type proved to be ideal for this formula, winning not only the up to £4500 class, but the first championship. Appropriately it was the V12 prototype, a 1969 fixed-head coupé that had started life with a 4.2-litre six-cylinder engine. Jaguar development engineer Peter Taylor bought it from the works after it had been converted

left
During the late nineteen-sixties, prod(uction) sports turned into mod(ified) sports car racing and 7 CXW changed its appeårance: wide wheels replaced the wire wheels of old; glass-fibre replaced the aluminium of the bonnet; but still she stormed on in the hands of strawberry farmer Rob Schroeder to gain many victories for Lenham Sports Cars

below
7 CXW in its final form in the green and yellow livery of Forward Engineering rather than the red and white of Lenham. It is pictured here in the hands of John Harper at Silverstone in 1971

to a series three E type in every way except the panel under the rear bumper, which remained pure series two. With stiffer dampers, reduced power assistance to the steering, and Michelin XWX tyres, he stormed away from all the opposition once a small problem with boiling brake fluid had been cured!

Meanwhile, in modsports, Guy Beddington, from Plymouth, was going fantastically fast in a fuel-injected V12 fixed-head coupé. Fuel injection wasn't officially allowed, but nobody seemed to mind. Perhaps they figured he wouldn't stay on the track too long and they needed a crowd puller now that plastic Pearson's XK was about to be outlawed because it had departed so far from original. Beddington and his mechanics spent countless hours perfecting the Tecalemit fuel injection to yield somewhere in the order of 500 bhp, but even in 1977 they were having trouble finishing a race; three hard applications of the brakes and they were no more, the car, which weighed only about a ton, was travelling so fast. You simply couldn't get enough cooling air to the brakes, a familiar Jaguar story.

The success and potential of these cars did not go

Yet another famous Jaguar . . . Sutcliffe's lightweight E type won a number of races in 1963 and 1964, and went to South Africa in 1965, never finishing lower than third in eight races entered. Sutcliffe sold it to Red Rose Motors via Richard Bond, where it acquired the name of Rosie, because of its paintwork. Richard Vincent was the next owner, followed by Bob Jennings, who, in turn, sold it to Mike MacDowel, then British hillclimb champion. MacDowel won numerous hillclimbs with Rosie before selling it to collector Brian Corser in 1968. Eventually Corser passed it on to fellow collector Walter Hill in Florida, via John Harper. Rosie is pictured here in the hands of Bob Jennings at a Blackbushe sprint in the mid-nineteen-sixties

unnoticed. A man called Bob Tullius persuaded British Leyland that racing a V12 would give a fillip to its flagging sales in the same way as Brennan's car had boosted sales so much in the mid-nineteen-sixties. The idea appealed to British Leyland, partly because of the excellent track record of Tullius's Virginia-based team and that of Huffaker Engineering in San Rafael, California, who had both been racing their products for years. In fact, Huffaker had been the man responsible for Brennan's car, and the Qvale lightweight before that. Using data supplied from Coventry by men such as Taylor, the SCCA E types needed only six months to be put into competitive trim.

They promptly wiped up the B production championship, with Tullius driving the Group 44 car and Lee Mueller moving over from Huffaker's MGB to his E type.

Three to four thousand man-hours went into the preparation of each car, with the teams comparing notes on difficult problems, eventually setting up each other's car, depending on local circuit knowledge. Not many of the lessons that Huffaker had learned on the Brennan car still applied; rules were much more restrictive in the nineteen-

One of the most successful modsports E type drivers throughout the nineteen-seventies was John Burbidge, pictured here at his home circuit, Thruxton, in 1976

Jaguar development engineer Peter Taylor powers his way to yet another victory in his V12 E type during his production sports car championship winning year, 1973

sixties. On the 1975 cars, the spring rates were nearly doubled at the front, with something like seventy-five per cent extra stiffness at the back. An additional anti-roll bar was fitted at the front with adjustments to vary the fore-and-aft pitch. The whole car was stripped, lowered and fitted with wide Minilite racing wheels and Goodyear tyres, with steering assistance reduced by thirty per cent.

Between 420 and 450 bhp was extracted from the V12 engine on regulation standard Stromberg carburetters and free exhaust; lap times resulted very much like those of a competitive Formula Ford.

Meanwhile, Roger Bighouse was achieving considerable success in SCCA C production events with a similarly modified, but 1966 model, 4.2-litre E type Roadster. This car, prepared by the Gran Turismo Jaguar dealership in Ohio, started winning races in 1973 and carried on after Group 44 and Huffaker had moved on to other British Leyland products in 1977, having dominated 1976 racing every bit as much as the year before.

Tyneside immigrant Fred Baker proved so successful in the Gran Turismo E type when he took over from Bighouse in 1977 that he began beating the A and B production cars, which were supposed to be faster, winning fourteen out of seventeen events in 1978! As all this has been going on, the factory lightweight E types are still being campaigned with great success in historic racing. There will never be another car quite like a racing E type, apart from its ancestor, the XK. It's a car for all seasons.

The ex-Cunningham E types are still top contenders in historic sports car racing. Here the Salvadori/Richards 1963 Le Mans car driven by American visitor Stephen Griswold takes Copse side by side with Cocks's Lotus 23B to finish fourth in the Jaguar Drivers' Club Silverstone spring meeting in 1977. The winner was Bobby Bell in a Lister-Jaguar

14
Leyland Cars
1
Leyland Cars
DUNLOP
DUNLOP

Chapter 8
The Big Cats

Wild enthusiasm greeted the Jaguar XJ competition coupé when it was first presented at Silverstone in March 1976. It subsequently spent that long hot summer slogging round the Grand Prix circuit in a search for strength, speed and stopping power. Even when it was standing still, taking a breather during one of these sessions, it looked full of aggression . . .

Everybody was thrilled when British Leyland announced in March 1977, Jaguar's return to racing. *Autosport* summed it up when they said: "This week is indeed a momentous one for British motor sport and its enthusiasts. Jaguar, the illustrious company which brought so much motor sport honour and pride to Britain in the 1950s, is back in racing. Leyland Cars, of which Jaguar is a part, have made complete their involvement in motor sport with this week's announcement of a full Jaguar racing programme for Europe.

"That Leyland should recognize that this move can positively help the company in marketing its products is a compliment to motor sport. We, in return, must wish them great success and give them every support in this very important and exciting adventure." Sadly, it all went wrong in Europe, although the crowds who saw the sensationally fast XJ twelve-cylinder coupés will never forget the sound, the fury and the succession of pole positions on grids from Silverstone to Czechoslovakia, from Nurburgring to Monza. British Leyland spent untold hundreds of thousands of pounds but were beset by internal politics in a troubled time, and the man in charge of development, Ralph Broad, suffered unforeseen setbacks, such as a family bereavement. Happily, the story was much more inspiring in America, where Group 44 moved on to the XJ-S coupé in 1976—and promptly mopped-up Category One in TransAm racing after their SCCA championship with the E type. Eventually Leyland quit racing Jaguars in Europe, but the Americans carry on with great success.

The XJ coupés for Europe were introduced with a great fanfare. The cars were built from their bare bodyshells to international Group Two specification with Broadspeed-developed engine, transmission and running gear. Contemporary Group Two specifications were a good deal

The competition coupé's power house. Twelve fuel injection trumpets, twelve-branch exhaust (six either side), high-mounted oil cooler, transistorized ignition, even the oil breather piping immaculately engineered by Ralph Broad

more liberal than they had been of late, allowing a racing car to be built from scratch instead of tacking on a hotch-potch of bits and pieces. With an exotic red, white and blue colour scheme the new Jaguar really looked the part: brutal, aggressive, an all-British racer ready to tear the throats out of the opposition, made up chiefly of German BMWs. These new Jaguars were as British as the BRM had been in 1950 and as fiercely nationalistic as Italian Ferraris have always been. Why, Jaguar even had their wide alloy wheels cast for them rather than use the popular German BBS line; and they had a lot of backing from the rest of British industry, just like BRM had so long before. Armstrong made them special competition shock absorbers so they didn't have to resort to the Dutch Konis, Lucas looked after the electrics and fuel injection, AP developed an incredible clutch that could take the near 600 bhp produced by Broadspeed's screaming twelve, SKF worked wonders with wheel bearings and Lockheed produced some truly exceptional brakes with no less than eight pots at the front. It all looked so good for Jaguar, but there were teething troubles that developed into severe toothache, such as the CSI governing body's refusal to allow dry sump lubrication, at first. So it was six months before a Jaguar turned its wheels in anger at the Tourist Trophy. Nevertheless, enthusiasm was still high as *Autosport* reported after a troublesome day at Silverstone in September:

"The Tourist Trophy is always a historic occasion, and last Sunday's event—the fortieth to be held in the famous history of the race, which goes back to 1905—had a particularly reminiscent atmosphere about it. This, of course, was due to the eagerly awaited debut of the Leyland Cars' Jaguar XJ12C. It was the first race appearance by a works-entered Jaguar for twenty years, and a fine crowd of 15,000, which is far more than can generally be expected by the promoters of modern endurance events, turned out in the hope that the new car could pull off Jaguar's first TT victory since those Stirling Moss triumphs of 1950 and 1951 at Dundrod.

"Such was the interest in the project that the British Racing Drivers' Club ran out of programmes on race morning, due purely to the Jaguar's pole position. For the TT sponsors, the Access credit card people, and for the BRDC, who had again illustrated the extent of their commitment at Silverstone by promoting an international meeting with uncertain crowd appeal, the Jaguar added an entirely new dimension to the event, a dimension of real spectator interest and involvement.

"During qualifying, the big Jaguar fulfilled all our hopes concerning noise and spectacle. In fact, coming out of the Woodcote chicane, it appeared to be in the advanced states of pregnancy and about to produce a litter at any moment, most probably somewhere in the vicinity of the paddock bridge. . . . With something approaching 600 bhp on tap and a race-ready weight of about thirty hundredweight, it looked desperately difficult to control, but on race day there it was, red, white and blue, a Union Jack on its driver's helmet and two whole seconds to the good in its endeavour to defeat the Hun. It was a fine sight.

"It failed, of course, but it failed with honour. Despite its eventual retirement, the Jaguar's performance exceeded the expectations of many motor racing people present, and the patriotic spectators went home fairly satisfied and dreaming of great things in 1977. Long live the Big Cat!"

Derek Bell had diced for the lead until the thirteenth lap, when a puncture forced him to drive more than two miles to the pits on a flat tyre. With a new wheel fitted, Bell fought back into the first fifteen before handing over to David Hobbs—then horror of horrors, the XJC lost a wheel; its race was over and its broken half shaft was blamed on Bell's enforced drive with the flat tyre. Jean Xhenceval and Pierre Dieudonne made it six victories in eight rounds to win the championship in their Luigi BMW 3.2 CSL from two more BMWs and an Alfa Romeo.

RH
B3

Meanwhile, in America, Group 44 had taken a radically different decision to Broad and British Leyland in that they were using the lighter XJ-S coupé. Starting late in the season, Tullius switched from his E type to take pole position before finishing fourth in class with the lap record in the Mosport TransAm race. In its next race, an SCCA national at Lime Rock, Tullius and the XJ-S again took pole position, but this time won the race besides setting a B production lap record. Their running gear was substantially the same as that developed by Broad except that they were using their own dry sump system—a feature that was to prove vital to the Big Cats. This dry sump system gave problems at the next SCCA race at Indianapolis and the XJ-S non-started—but when Tullius's three wins in the E type were added to the one win in the XJ-S that year, he qualified for the SCCA finals at Road Atlanta. "And there, against the best B production cars in the country, Tullius qualified the XJ-S almost a second quicker than the fastest of the Corvette contingent. But a first-lap spin and a seventh-lap fire put the immaculately prepared Jag coupé on the sidelines and denied Tullius his sixth national title," reported *Road & Track*. Nevertheless, he set a lap record of 98.65 mph and 1977 looked full of promise for the racing Jaguar coupés on both sides of the Atlantic.

above
As the pace car dived for cover, Derek Bell powered away into the lead with the XJ coupé in its first race, the 1976 Tourist Trophy at Silverstone. But Gunnar Nilsson fought back with the faster of Luigi's two BMW "Batmobiles", with Stuart Graham's Chevrolet Camaro rumbling round on his tail

left
How do you stop one and a half tons doing more than 180 mph within a pitifully few metres? With difficulty and massive eight-pot front brake calipers fitted to the Jaguar competition coupé. These were Ralph Broad's eventual solution to what must have been one of his most formidable problems

On the second lap, Nilsson outbraked the XJC at the chicane, but Bell chased grimly, cornering on three wheels and staying in front of the menacing Camaro

Considerable development took place on the XJC throughout the winter, but two serious weaknesses were to show themselves in the coming season: weak drive shafts (the lesson of Silverstone had not been learned) and inadequate lubrication with the wet sump system, despite a complex series of baffles. A big engine like the bored-out 5.4-litre V12 needed a delivery rate of 1800 gallons of oil an hour. The lubrication problem reared its ugly head in the first round of the 1977 European Touring Car Championship at Monza in March. Heavy braking for slow chicanes set up at the request of the Formula One track users forced the V12 engine's oil to the front of the sump and starved the rearmost of the numerous bearings. The British Leyland team blew two engines like this in practice and fitted their spare to Fitzpatrick's car. Mechanics from the rival Alpina BMW team helped Broad's men fit a modified baffle system since they had had similar problems before; BMW were of the opinion that it wasn't worth racing without Jaguar opposition, so they were just as keen for the Big Cats to make the grid as Leyland. The Alpina modifications partially helped to cure the oil surge problem and Fitzpatrick promptly took pole position with one glorious flat-out lap; after that he just toured round in practice, conserving the engine. It was also the first time the team had had the chance to test their tyres on a track at a reasonable

By lap five of the 1976 TT, Bell had taken the lead again, but Nilsson took him on lap nine, the Jaguar suffering from tyre trouble—it needed three different compounds, one for the front wheels and one each side at the back! Soon one of its rear tyres gave way and Bell had a long drive back to the pits, the flailing rubber leaving the rim in the end, giving the car a terrible hammering. Five laps were lost in the pits as Broad's men frantically fought to change the wheel. Headlights blazing, Bell then re-entered the fray, to take revenge on Nilsson's BMW, which had also suffered a flat tyre. The British car overtook the Belgian-entered BMW once more, setting a Group Two lap record of 1 minute 38.5 seconds (107.15 mph) in the process, and scattering Stuart Rolt's Ford Capri and John Fitzpatrick's second-placed BMW in its wake. But it was all in vain—the Jaguar lost a wheel and Nilsson's team-mates, Jean Xhenceval, Pierre Dieudonne and Hughes de Fierlant, won

By the end of the next year, 1977, the XJ coupés had acquired more blue paint—on the sides—a different front air dam, new rear spoiler, no end of changes under the skin, and a reputation second to none for lap records and unreliability—which Broad's foreman, Andy Rouse, is trying to eradicate here while testing at Silverstone

temperature; it had been a long, cold winter in Britain. In the race itself, Fitzpatrick led for the first fifty minutes before handing over to Australian Tim Schenken; only two laps later the V12 tightened up and the race was over for the XJC.

A despondent Ralph Broad said that a combination of short-sighted CSI officials banning dry-sump lubrication and F1CA officials insisting on chicanes for their drivers had effectively put paid to Leyland's chances in the championship. He was later to claim that equally short-sighted decisions by his own sponsors were to blame for drive shaft failures which proved to be the Big Cats' Achilles' heel. Apparently the flanges of the drive shafts needed expensive re-engineering to stand the strain of the cars' enormous performance. So Broad started lobbying on two fronts: one with the CSI to get dry sumping allowed for the Group Two cars, and the other for re-engineered drive shafts. When the Germans backed Broad, the CSI started to waver, but he met with sterner resistance from British Leyland. The programme had cost a fortune already and they were struggling to justify the expenditure of taxpayers'

money; besides, it had always been agreed that the XJC racing programme would not interfere with the company's already busy engineering programme.

With these twin problems unsolved, the XJCs headed for Salzburgring in Austria for the second round of the championship two weeks later. Things looked good at first. One Jaguar took pole position in practice during a brief dry spell with the other alongside. But this time, they lasted only forty minutes of the three-and-a-half-hour race. Andy Rouse was leading Dieter Quester's Alpina BMW when third-placed Schenken came into the pits with a broken drive shaft flange. It was only natural to check the flanges on the leading car when it pitted with a holed radiator—and it was found that they, too, were cracking. Obviously it would have been foolhardy to have continued, and BMW went on to win, as they had done at Monza.

The Jaguar team returned home bitterly disappointed and Broad now had enough ammunition to force the issue over the drive shafts. But new drive shafts are not made in a day; they took all week and initial testing could not start until 1 May. Several problems cropped up and took

What is this world if full of care, there is no time to stand and stare? Time was running out for the Jaguar competition coupé as it underwent yet more tests at Silverstone, all muffled up against the British climate. Why all the grille space at the front then? It gets awfully hot at Monza . . .

Rouse did most of the testing on Jaguar's home circuit, Silverstone, so it was hardly surprising that he set the fastest time in practice for the 1977 Tourist Trophy with the wet sump XJC

another five days to solve; too late to qualify for the next round at Mugello. The cars were also withdrawn from the fourth round at Enna on 22 May in the hope that they could be perfected and there would be no repeat of the previous débâcles. Meanwhile, pressure was building up on the CSI to relent over dry sumping. The Alpina team backed Jaguars in refusing to enter for Enna, putting the whole series in jeopardy.

With this stormy political backdrop, Broad got down to some serious testing, culminating in full four-hour sessions at Goodwood, notorious for its tight corners and exhausting for the drivers. But the cars, fitted with the new drive shafts, came through these tests with flying colours; it was the sort of session that they had wanted to do for months, but had been unable to attempt because of an unusually severe winter.

Fitzpatrick and Tim Schenken tried hard in the dry sump car, too—but they could manage one second place in practice, fractions of a second faster than three BMWs. The dry sump car ran cooler, hence the slight grille blanking here

So it was with considerable confidence that they faced the fifth round at Brno in Czechoslovakia; they gained pole position as usual and Fitzpatrick led for the first seven laps. Then a tyre exploded and ripped out so much of the rear end that a rebuild was needed. As if this wasn't enough for the overworked mechanics, Bell needed a new oil pipe to replace one that had split. Both cars rejoined the race after an hour, but Bell succumbed to gearbox failure, leaving Fitzpatrick and Schenken to thunder on in their battered car. Towards the end they were struggling with a slipping clutch, too, but they brought home the Big Cat in sixteenth place; they had finished a race at last and there was hope for the future! BMWs won of course.

Then the CSI relented and allowed dry sumping, despite opposition from French and Italian teams who didn't want the Germans and British to disappear further into the distance. However, by this time, Broad had mixed feelings about the value of dry sumping. It was enormously expensive to develop and he had had enough trouble already over money. Besides, he had improved the wet sump system so much that it was coping quite well by Brno. He felt, therefore, that if he was to use dry sump equipment, it would have to be proved to be superior to his revised wet sumping and because of the expense, his dry sump system had progressed no further than the design stage, so far.

Schenken stormed into the lead in the TT in front of Rouse and Dieter Quester's Alpina BMW, followed by the Luigi BMWs. Jaguars had started as they meant to finish . . .

But Schenken's lead was short-lived, for on the fourth lap he lost the Jaguar on oil deposited by Tony Dron's Triumph Dolomite, and Rouse took the lead from a phalanx of BMWs. Soon Schenken fought back through the serried ranks of BMWs to take his rightful station alongside his team-mate by lap seven, with a hundred to go . . .

Therefore, the XJCs went to the Nurburgring for the sixth round in mid-July with wet sumps. British Leyland hired the circuit for a whole day before practice so that the mechanics could sort out the complex wet sumping system; it needed patient tuning to cater for the myriad bends of that famous circuit. As the race drew close, Broad said they had lost count of the times they had changed engines—but the exhausted team, who had gone through repeated ten-hour engine swops, head gasket and wheel balance troubles, were rewarded with yet another pole position for Fitzpatrick.

He shot off into the lead in the race itself to break the lap record with the might of Germany trailing; at last a Jaguar was Lord of the Ring. No sooner had he completed this lap than his wet sump cried enough; but Bell was easing off fourth place behind three BMWs. Then two of them pitted and Bell was left chasing Quester's BeeEm. As the race wore on Gunnar Nilsson took over from Quester, and Rouse from Bell; the BMW's oil pressure dropped and, in the dying laps, Bell halved the BMW's lead to finish second only three minutes down. The times they were a-changing for Jaguars. They were competitive on the world's toughest road circuit for the first time ever.

The seventh round at Zandvoort was tame by comparison. Quester won again—with Hezemans, after being

ALPINA
Mobil
Gösser

Soon it was Jaguar-Jaguar-BMW again with the green Alpina-Gosser Bier car best of the Bavarians. Then rain began to fall and the Big Cats became a handful in front of the lithe nineteen-hundredweight BMW

The green BMW got past Schenken and became sandwiched behind Rouse as they lapped the tail end of the field. On the thirty-sixth lap, Quester was almost in the boot of the leading Jaguar, with Schenken not far behind and about to stop for fuel. But Schenken, pictured here, never got there. His car lost a wheel at Becketts . . .

harried by Rouse in a wet-sump XJC; he had tyre trouble before blowing up his differential. Fitzpatrick had the other XJC—fitted with Broad's brand new dry sump system—which lacked development and suffered from repeated oil pump drive failure, giving the mechanics more nightmares as they kept it going to the finish. It was so far behind, though, that it was unclassified.

It was make or break for the Big Cats in the eighth round, the TT at Silverstone in September. Twenty thousand people turned up to cheer them on, willing the Jaguars to win. Once again they occupied pole position with Rouse fastest in the wet sump car he shared with Bell. For thirty-six laps of the 107-lap race he disputed the lead with Quester's BMW and Schenken in the dry sump XJC. Then Schenken lost a wheel—shades of the previous year—and the wet sump car battled on, never far apart from the BeeEm till Rouse lost it on a patch of oil with less than ten laps to go. Once more, Jaguars' race was run, although it had gone so fast it was still classified fourth; fourth when it could have been first, there seemed no end to the bad luck as the disappointed crowds streamed home.

Pit stops were of prime importance to the Jaguar competition coupés with their fuel consumption as low as 4.5 mpg during a race . . . twin fuel fillers were fitted in the boot, an anti-crash precaution developed following a fiery and nearly fatal accident to Peter Proctor when the fuel filler of his Ford Anglia ruptured in a crash at Brands Hatch years before . . . with the bootlid shut, the fillers were still accessible, yet were still part of the tank

Leyland
2

Leyland
2

It needed only another failure in the ninth round at Zolder—Fitzpatrick and Schenken out with a dropped valve, Bell and Rouse sidelined with a broken gearbox, all within ninety minutes—for Leyland to cry enough; we had seen the last of what was potentially the most spectacular Jaguar ever. Once again, *Autosport* summed it all up:

"Miaouw! Last Sunday the Big Cats suffered more humiliation in Belgium when they failed yet again in a European Touring Car Championship race. The following day, the briefest of statements declared the withdrawal of the Broadspeed-prepared Leyland Cars Jaguars from the remaining three races of the Group Two series. Finally, the nearest thing we had to a national racing team has gone down the drain, along with a great deal of public money. We have not a single victory to show for all the effort and expense.

"Starting with the original announcement of the Group Two project (which was disgracefully premature), the story has been one of unremitting failure. We will admit that, because of the patriotic nature of the project at a time when Britain's international reputation has been at a low ebb, it

The surviving Jaguar completed its two pit stops to the BMW's one and set off with Rouse taking over from Bell to try to cut Walkinshaw's twenty-two-second lead with thirty laps to go. But Tom Walkinshaw was as fast in the BMW as Quester had been, and Rouse could only reduce the gap to thirteen seconds with nine laps to go. He lost the Big Cat on yet another patch of oil and Jaguar's hopes of ever winning the European Touring Car Championship went spinning into the catchfencing. "Had we have been able to have won at Silverstone, we might have been able to carry on," said Broad. As it was they could only watch the green BMW roar on to win. Later Walkinshaw admitted that he nearly lost it on the same oil patch, but his car weighed only two-thirds that of the Jaguar. And that, more than anything, is why the Big Cat failed

has not received the criticism it has deserved within the pages of *Autosport*. But it must be said that the basic problem—that the XJ5.3C was essentially unsuitable for advanced competition development—should have been recognized at the outset.

"There will be those who will disagree, and point to the admittedly fine record of pole positions and fastest race laps. But we will contend that the Jaguar was too bulky and heavy to be seriously seen as a full-race saloon car. We will point out that, apart from the engine, competition development was never considered in the basic design of the XJ5.3C. We will draw attention to the standard of the opposition. And we will wonder at the wisdom of a factory team which races a model soon to be phased out of production.

"The purpose of it all was to promote Leyland's corporate image. We believe that the image which the programme was designed to convey is right for Leyland, and it is our hope that the company will embark on a new racing project of similar prestige. It is also our hope that the company resists the temptation to do so in 1978.

"The Leyland competitions department—let alone Leyland executive management—does not now need to be told of the dangers of failure. The dismal Jaguar results (which bear no reflection on the ability and dedication of the team drivers) have tended to overshadow other aspects of the Leyland competition programme. . . ."

What a way to go; it would have been tragic had it not been for the unremitting success of the XJ-S in America. The 1977 Group 44 car went even better than before in TransAm racing. All their energies were concentrated on this car, rather than divided among the four cars they had been running in SCCA amateur events. And it paid off! Tullius won five out of the ten TransAm Category One professional races in which they competed despite tough opposition from Porsche and Chevrolet Corvettes.

"We did a lot with the aerodynamics and we strengthened the car," Tullius told *Jaguar Journal*. "Racing an hour-long race or longer, opposed to a half-hour race, we had to do things that we hadn't done with the car prior to that. We fabricated stronger hubs and some stronger rear axles and we had more of an assortment of gear ratios. We ducted the brakes a whole lot better. We improved the cockpit ventilation substantially. We didn't want to have any more broiling-turkey drivers. We did a lot of work in the weight distribution to make the rear end heavier."

For the record, they won at Seattle; Westwood, British Columbia; Hallett, Oklahoma; Mosport, Ontario; and Road America, Wisconsin, with second place at Brainerd, Minnesota, and third at St Jovite, Montreal. Seattle was

The XJ-S of Bob Tullius and Group 44, pictured here at Mosport in 1976, looks remarkably standard compared with the Chevrolet Corvette chasing it. Its V12 engined 475 bhp using six 44 mm Weber carburetters and dry sump lubrication. Stock power steering and gearbox were used with Lockheed disc brakes for the front wheels and a triple-plate clutch (the rear brakes were Jaguar's own). Its appearance differed mainly because of the tyres, $24\frac{1}{2} \times 10$ inch front and 27×11 inch rear, and full NASCAR-style roll cage

won in the rain, Westwood yielded fastest lap, as did Portland, Oregon, before retirement with gearbox trouble; fastest lap followed again at Nelson Lodges, Ohio, before ignition failure when leading by forty-five seconds with only three laps to go. Fourth place followed in the Watkins Glen six hour after wheel, brake and battery bothers, followed by fastest lap and first place at Hallett. Yet another fastest lap was chalked up at Brainerd before a broken piston ring slowed the Jaguar to second place. Co-driver Brian Fuerstenau, who had been responsible for much of the preparation and development of the XJ-S, did a good job to help Tullius to win the Mosport six hour, before the XJ-S passed all the leaders to win the second day of the Road America races. Bad vibrations relegated it to third place in the final race at St Jovite.

But there were no bad vibrations from Alex Park, then chief executive of Leyland, when he heard the results. He was overjoyed! "We were absolutely delighted to hear Bob Tullius's good news in the TransAm championship," he said. "It is a marvellous victory and is the kind of tonic we need for our motor racing programme." At last the V12 had proved itself in competition as all the Jaguars before it.

BRITISH LEYLAND
44
QUAKER STATE
XJS

This shot of the Group 44/Quaker State Jaguar XJ-S shows how racing cars can differ in detail specification. Note the five extra front/side-mounted bonnet (hood) pins, deeper front spoiler, rectangular headlamp surrounds (apparently to European specification), wider front and rear wheel arches with squared-off effect, windscreen centre brace and open side lamp housings for better cooling

Bibliography

Books

Behind the Wheel David McKay (Ure Smith) Sydney, 1960
Challenge Me The Race Mike Hawthorn (William Kimber) London, 1958
Champion Year Mike Hawthorn (William Kimber) London, 1959
Climax in Coventry Walter Hassan and Graham Robson (MRP) London, 1975
E type: End of an Era Chris Harvey (Oxford Illustrated Press) Oxford, 1977
Ecurie Ecosse David Murray (Stanley Paul) London, 1962
Jaguar Sports Cars Paul Skilleter (Foulis) Somerset, England 1975
John Cooper: Grand Prix Carpetbagger John Cooper with John Bentley (Doubleday) New York, 1977
Life at the Limit Graham Hill (William Kimber) London, 1969
The Jaguar XK Chris Harvey (Oxford Illustrated Press) Oxford, 1978
The Le Mans 24-Hour Race Automobile Club de l'Ouest (Edita) Switzerland, 1974
The Sebring Story Alec Ulmann (Chilton) New York, 1969
Touch Wood! Duncan Hamilton (Barrie and Rockliff) London, 1960

Magazines

Autocar, (The) (British)
Autosport (British)
Cars and Car Conversions (British)
CAR (British)
Car and Driver (American)
Cars Illustrated (British)
Cat-a-Log (Australian)
Jaguar Driver (British)
Jaguar Journal (American)
Jaguar Journal (British)
Motor, (The) (British)
Motor Sport (British)
Motor Racing (British)
Motoring News (British)
Practical Motorist (British)
Road & Track (American)
Sports Cars Illustrated (American)
Sports Cars Illustrated (British)
Sports Car Graphic (American)
Sports Car World (Australian)
Sporting Motorist (British)
Thoroughbred and Classic Cars (British)

Index